THE **100** MOST
IMPORTANT
BIBLE VERSES
FOR DEALING WITH
ANXIETY
AND FEAR

SMITH FREEMAN Publishing

Table of Contents by Topic

A MESSAGE TO READERS

Anxiety and fear. These two emotional reactions have the power to invade our lives and hijack our thoughts. And there's no question that as citizens of the twenty-first century, we are continually subjected to a steady stream of anxiety-producing, fear-provoking messages that can leave us breathless. So what should we do in response? For starters, we should turn to God's Word for guidance and comfort.

This book contains one hundred essential Bible verses that are intended to help you deal with anxiety, with fear, and with other negative emotions that have the potential to do you harm. If you find yourself focusing on your fears instead of God's promises, the ideas on these pages will provide the wisdom, the courage, and the practical advice you'll need for managing your thoughts and improving your outlook.

The Lord has given you a guidebook for spiritual, emotional, physical, and psychological health. That book, of course, is the Holy Bible. The Bible is a priceless gift, an infallible tool that God intends for you to use every day, in good times and in hard times. Your intentions should be the same.

When you weave the Lord's message into the fabric of your day—when you learn to focus more intently on His promises and less intently on your fears—you'll quickly discover that God's Word has the power to change everything, including your attitude. So if you sincerely desire to find better strategies for dealing with anxiety and fear, keep searching for direction: God's direction. When you do, you'll discover the courage, the comfort, the peace that only He can give.

YOU ARE NOT ALONE

If your life has been impacted by feelings of anxiety or fear, you are not alone. Please consider the following:

- Anxiety disorders are the most common mental illness in the United States.
- An estimated 19.1 percent of US adults have experienced an anxiety disorder during the past year.
- An estimated 31.1 percent of US adults will experience an anxiety disorder at some time in their lives.

- Anxiety disorders are highly treatable, yet only 36.9 percent of those suffering receive treatment.*

So what should these statistics mean to you? For starters, the fact that feelings of anxiety and fear are commonplace means that treatment options are commonplace too. So if you're feeling anxious, worried, fretful, or afraid, you need not suffer alone. Help is readily available.

Furthermore, the fact that almost one-third of your fellow citizens will experience an anxiety disorder at some point in their lives means that you can feel free to talk openly about your situation. When you share your anxious feelings with others, you'll undoubtedly be speaking to people who have either experienced anxiety themselves or have seen its impact on close friends or family members.

Finally, and most importantly, you must remember that even in your darkest moments, God is with you. He never leaves you; He never stops loving you; and He always keeps His promises. So when you walk through life's darkest valleys, you can be certain that you will never walk alone. The Lord will be with you, and He is always available.

As you consider ways to deal with anxiety and fear, please remember that you don't have to find solutions by yourself. You can seek help from family, from friends, from your pastor, from your physician, or from all of them. And while you're at it, you can ask God to guide you and protect you. When you do these things, you can rest assured that help is on the way. Fast.

*Sources: The National Institute of Mental Health and the Anxiety and Depression Association of America.

Ten Essential Steps for Dealing with Anxiety and Fear

Accept the fact that chronic negative emotions such as anxiety and fear can be dangerous to your mental, spiritual, and physical health. God wants you to experience the abundant life that He describes in John 10:10. To achieve it, you must guard your heart and mind against irrational worries, anxieties, and fears.

Understand that it's possible to control irrational fears and anxieties. If you believe that you have no control over your anxieties and fears, you're wrong. It may take training, education, practice, and, in some cases, medication. But if you sincerely desire to gain better control over these negative emotions, you can do it. With God, all things are possible.

When you experience a major life-altering change or a significant loss, express your feelings honestly. If you're experiencing a life-changing event, or if you're recovering from a recent loss, don't keep everything bottled up inside. Talk to people you can trust and express your feelings. And while you're at it, remember that God promises to heal the brokenhearted. In time, He will heal your heart and dry your tears if you let Him. So if you haven't already allowed Him to begin His healing process, today is a perfect day to start.

Understand that negative emotions are highly contagious. Unless you make the conscious effort to take control of your thoughts and emotions, other people's outbursts can add to your fears and anxieties. If you find yourself in a situation where another person's negative emotions are continually infecting yours, ask God to help you guard your heart. And while you're at it, establish as much physical and psychological distance as you can by establishing clear boundaries between yourself and the difficult person.

Identify any stimulants or medications that may be contributing to your anxiety. Sometimes anxieties and irrational fears can be triggered by chemical substances. For example, high-caffeine drinks, when consumed in sufficient quantities, can make you feel anxious, even when you have little or nothing to feel anxious about. Additionally, many medications have side effects that can cause fearful or anxious feelings. So if you're taking medication—or if you're consuming large amounts of caffeine or high-energy drinks—please understand that the chemicals in those substances may be contributing to your emotional distress.

Monitor your media intake. Traditional media and social media share a common goal: to capture your attention and keep you engaged on their platforms. Various media outlets may use disturbing content, anger-inducing narratives, inappropriate images, gratuitous violence, or sensationalized news to keep you tuned in. So whether you realize it or not, the media may be adding to your anxieties and fears. The answer to this dilemma, of course, is to monitor your media intake and to act accordingly.

Avoid the pitfalls of procrastination. Procrastination breeds worry; worry breeds anxiety; anxiety breeds fear; fear breeds more procrastination, and the cycle continues. If you're constantly putting off until tomorrow what should be done today, you're actually manufacturing things to worry about. A far better strategy is undoubtedly this: tackle today's problems *today* so that you don't have to worry about them *tomorrow*.

Forgive everybody. Hate and peace cannot coexist in the same human heart. God's Word makes it clear that if you want to experience the peace that passes all understanding—His peace— you must learn how to forgive and move on with your life. So the sooner you forgive everybody—including yourself—the sooner you'll begin feeling better about yourself and your world.

Get plenty of rest. Most adults need about eight hours of sleep each night. If you're constantly depriving yourself of much-needed sleep, you may be harming your overall health while manufacturing needless stress and anxiety. So if you've acquired the habit of staying up late and robbing yourself of sleep, it's time to establish a new (and better) habit by turning off your devices and going to bed. But what if you're simply too anxious or too worried to fall asleep or to stay asleep? If you can't sleep, talk with your physician about your sleeping patterns, your situation, your habits, and your emotional state. You need a good night's sleep to think clearly and realistically about your life, your blessings, and God's love.

If your emotions—or the emotions of someone you love—begin to spiral out of control, seek professional help immediately. Small emotional swings are an inevitable part of everyday life. But dramatic emotional swings—such as intense feelings of anxiety, despair, panic, or fear—are dangerous. So don't be embarrassed to seek professional help. Mental health professionals have numerous tools at their disposal to help you deal with emotional swings and anxiety disorders. Since help is available, you should ask for it as soon as you detect a problem.

1

ANXIETY AND FEAR

So humble yourselves under the mighty power of God,
and at the right time he will lift you up in honor.
Give all your worries and cares to God, for he cares about you.
Stay alert! Watch out for your great enemy, the devil.
He prowls around like a roaring lion, looking for someone
to devour. Stand firm against him, and be strong in your faith.
Remember that your family of believers all over the world
is going through the same kind of suffering you are.

1 PETER 5:6–9 NLT

Ours is an anxious generation. Never before have so many people been inundated with so much information that has the potential to create so much fear, so much anxiety, and so much dread. On average, adults consume approximately five times more information each day than did their counterparts fifty years ago. In fact, a recent survey found that the typical American spends over eleven hours per day listening to, watching, reading, or interacting with some form of media. No wonder so many of us feel like anxious observers, watching helplessly as the world spins out of control.

Sometimes our anxieties and fears also have physiological origins. Too much caffeine, for example, can heighten anxious feelings. And sometimes medications can have unintended side effects that can make us feel nervous.

Exercise, diet, and sleep can also affect our emotions. Regular exercise can reduce stress; a sensible diet promotes good overall health; and common-sense sleep habits have numerous benefits that impact both mind and body.

So if you're serious about dealing with anxiety and fear, you should monitor your media consumption, your medications, your sleep, and your diet. You should also determine the level of exercise that's right for you. But that's not the end of the story. If you're seeking permanent peace—God's peace—then you should also examine your ongoing relationship with Him.

God loves you and wants the best for you. He sent His Son so that you might experience the gift of eternal life. And during your sojourn from cradle to grave, He remains a constant resource, never leaving you, not even for an instant. The Lord is always present, always attentive, and always available. When you're feeling anxious or afraid, you can take your concerns to Him in prayer, and that's precisely what you should do.

So the next time you're feeling nervous, edgy, or worse, remember that anxiety and panic are temporary conditions that you and God, working together, can manage. When you do your part, He will most certainly do His.

MORE THOUGHTS ABOUT ANXIETY, FEAR, AND FAITH

The closer you live to God, the smaller everything else appears.
RICK WARREN

Since the Lord is your shepherd, what are you worried about?
MARIE T. FREEMAN

What you trust to Him you must not worry over nor feel anxious about. Trust and worry cannot go together.

HANNAH WHITALL SMITH

MORE FROM GOD'S WORD

Let not your heart be troubled; you believe in God, believe also in Me.

JOHN 14:1 NKJV

Therefore don't worry about tomorrow, because tomorrow will worry about itself. Each day has enough trouble of its own.

MATTHEW 6:34 HCSB

Be anxious for nothing, but in everything by prayer and supplication, with thanksgiving, let your requests be made known to God.

PHILIPPIANS 4:6 NKJV

Those who trust in the LORD are as secure as Mount Zion; they will not be defeated but will endure forever.

PSALM 125:1 NLT

A TIMELY TIP

When it comes to solving problems, work beats worry and trust beats anxiety. So instead of fretting about your troubles, get busy tackling the problems that you can solve, and turn everything else over to the Lord.

2

ASKING FOR HELP

DON'T BE AFRAID TO ASK FOR HELP

Get all the advice and instruction you can,
so you will be wise the rest of your life.
PROVERBS 19:20 NLT

If you're experiencing intense feelings of anxiety or fear, you don't have to suffer alone. Help is always available, and you should ask for it. No matter how much you think you know about your emotional state, it never hurts to hear an informed opinion from a knowledgeable professional. By expressing your feelings to a pastoral counselor, to a therapist, to a psychologist, or to your physician, you can gain knowledge about your condition and you can learn better ways to deal with your feelings and your fears.

When you talk to someone who understands the physical and psychological triggers that are causing your emotional pain, you can learn better coping strategies, better ways to react to the world around you, and better ways to think about your circumstances and your future.

The Roman playwright Plautus said, "None of us are wise enough by ourselves." What was true in 200 BC is still true today. In today's complicated world, we all need the benefit of good counsel, informed opinions, and honest advice, especially when we're dealing with painful emotions.

More Thoughts about Asking for Help

God guides through the counsel of good people.
E. STANLEY JONES

*It takes a wise person to give good advice,
but an even wiser person to take it.*
MARIE T. FREEMAN

*The next best thing to being wise oneself
is to live in a circle of those who are.*
C. S. LEWIS

*Do not be inaccessible. None is so perfect that
he does not need at times the advice of others.*
BALTASAR GRACIÁN

He that won't be counseled can't be helped.
BEN FRANKLIN

*The effective mentor strives to help a man or woman
discover what they can be in Christ and then
holds them accountable to become that person.*
HOWARD HENDRICKS

More from God's Word

The wise are glad to be instructed.
PROVERBS 10:8 NLT

He whose ear listens to the life-giving reproof will dwell among the wise.
PROVERBS 15:31 NASB

How much better is it to get wisdom than gold! and to get understanding rather to be chosen than silver!
PROVERBS 16:16 KJV

Plans fail when there is no counsel, but with many advisers they succeed.
PROVERBS 15:22 HCSB

Spend time with the wise and you will become wise, but the friends of fools will suffer.
PROVERBS 13:20 NCV

A Timely Tip

If you're experiencing high anxiety or debilitating fear, don't keep everything bottled up inside, and don't be embarrassed to ask for help. Find people you can talk to and, if necessary, experienced professionals you can trust. A second opinion (or, for that matter, a third or fourth opinion) can be helpful.

3

ASKING GOD

ASK GOD FOR THE THINGS YOU NEED

Ask, and it will be given to you; seek, and you will find;
knock, and it will be opened to you. For everyone
who asks receives, and he who seeks finds,
and to him who knocks it will be opened.

MATTHEW 7:7-8 NASB

If you're dealing with roller-coaster emotions, you need God's help. And if you ask Him, He will most certainly provide the help you need. So how often do you ask the Lord for His help and His wisdom? Occasionally? Intermittently? Whenever you experience a crisis? Hopefully not. Hopefully you've acquired the habit of asking for God's assistance early and often. And hopefully you have learned to seek His guidance in every aspect of your life.

Jesus made it clear to His disciples: they should petition God to meet their needs. So should you. Genuine, heartfelt prayer produces powerful changes in you and in your world. God can do great things through you if you have the courage to ask Him (and the determination to keep asking Him). But don't expect Him to do all the work. When you do your part, He will do His part—and when He does, you can expect miracles to happen.

The Bible promises that God will guide you if you let Him. Your job is to let Him. But sometimes you will be tempted to do otherwise. Sometimes you'll be tempted to go along with the crowd, even when the crowd is heading in the wrong direction. Other times, you'll be tempted to do things your way, not God's way. When you feel those temptations, resist them. Instead, ask the Lord to lead you, to protect you, and to correct you. Then trust the answers He gives.

God stands at the door and waits. When you knock, He opens. When you ask, He answers. Your task, of course, is to make God a full partner in every aspect of your life—and to seek His guidance prayerfully, confidently, and often.

Asking God for the Things You Need

God will help us become the people we are meant to be, if only we will ask Him.
HANNAH WHITALL SMITH

God insists that we ask, not because He needs to know our situation, but because we need the spiritual discipline of asking.
CATHERINE MARSHALL

It's important that you keep asking God to show you what He wants you to do. If you don't ask, you won't know.
STORMIE OMARTIAN

We honor God by asking for great things when they are a part of His promise. We dishonor Him and cheat ourselves when we ask for molehills where He has promised mountains.

VANCE HAVNER

MORE FROM GOD'S WORD

Do not be anxious about anything,
but in every situation, by prayer and petition,
with thanksgiving, present your requests to God.
PHILIPPIANS 4:6 NIV

You did not choose me, but I chose you and appointed you so that you might go and bear fruit—fruit that will last— and so that whatever you ask in my name the Father will give you.
JOHN 15:16 NIV

Until now you have asked for nothing in My name. Ask and you will receive, that your joy may be complete.
JOHN 16:24 HCSB

The effective prayer of a righteous man can accomplish much.
JAMES 5:16 NASB

A TIMELY TIP

If you're experiencing anxieties or fears, ask for God's help. And remember that if you have questions, God has answers. So when in doubt, pray. And keep praying until the answers arrive.

4

ASSURANCE

This is the confidence we have in approaching God:
that if we ask anything according to his will, he hears us.
1 JOHN 5:14 NIV

Sometimes, amid the demands and the frustrations of everyday life, we forget to slow ourselves down long enough to talk with God. Instead of turning our thoughts and prayers to Him, we rely upon our own resources. Instead of praying for emotional strength and courage, we seek to manufacture these things by ourselves. Instead of asking God for guidance, we depend only upon our own limited wisdom. Instead of trusting Him completely, we look elsewhere for assurance.

God has made many promises, and He intends to keep every one of them. Our job, simply put, is to trust and obey.

Fanny Crosby spoke for believers of every generation when, in her hymn "Blessed Assurance," she wrote these lines:

Blessed assurance, Jesus is mine!
O what a foretaste of glory divine!
Heir of salvation, purchase of God,
Born of his Spirit, washed in his blood.

This is my story, this is my song,
Praising my Savior, all the day long;
This is my story, this is my song,
Praising my Savior all the day long.

So the next time you find your courage tested to the limit, lean upon God's promises. Trust His Son. Remember that God is always near and that He is your protector and your deliverer. When you are worried, anxious, or afraid, call upon Him. God can handle your troubles infinitely better than you can, so turn them over to Him. Remember that God rules both mountaintops and valleys with limitless wisdom and love, now and forever.

MORE THOUGHTS ABOUT ASSURANCE

Faith is the assurance that the thing which
God has said in His Word is true, and that
God will act according to what He has said.
GEORGE MUELLER

Only believe, don't fear. Our Master, Jesus,
always watches over us, and no matter what
the persecution, Jesus will surely overcome it.
LOTTIE MOON

I refuse to become panicky, as I lift up my eyes to Him
and accept it as coming from the throne of God
for some great purpose of blessing to my own heart.
ALAN REDPATH

As you walk through the valley of the unknown, you will find
the footprints of Jesus both in front of you and beside you.
CHARLES STANLEY

MORE FROM GOD'S WORD

Let us hold fast the confession of our hope without wavering,
for He who promised is faithful.
HEBREWS 10:23 NASB

Great is thy faithfulness.
LAMENTATIONS 3:23 KJV

For the LORD is good; His mercy is everlasting,
and His truth endures to all generations.
PSALM 100:5 NKJV

Sustain me as You promised, and I will live;
do not let me be ashamed of my hope.
PSALM 119:116 HCSB

They will bind themselves to the LORD with an eternal
covenant that will never be forgotten.
JEREMIAH 50:5 NLT

A TIMELY TIP

God has promised to protect you, and He's going to keep that
promise. So if you're worried or afraid, pray about it. And as you're
praying, be mindful that your Father is always faithful.

5

ATTITUDE

MAINTAIN THE RIGHT KIND OF ATTITUDE

You must have the same attitude that Christ Jesus had.
PHILIPPIANS 2:5 NLT

Attitudes are the mental filters through which we view and interpret the world around us. Positive attitudes produce positive emotions; negative attitudes don't.

The quality of your attitude will help determine the quality of your life, so you must guard your thoughts accordingly. If you make up your mind to approach life with a healthy mixture of realism and optimism, you'll be rewarded. But if you allow yourself to fall into the unfortunate habit of negative thinking, you will doom yourself to unhappiness, or mediocrity, or worse.

So the next time you find yourself dwelling upon the negative aspects of your life, refocus your attention on things positive. The next time you find yourself falling prey to the blight of pessimism, stop yourself and turn your thoughts around. The next time you're tempted to waste valuable time gossiping or complaining or revisiting past misfortunes, resist those temptations. Count your blessings instead of your hardships. And thank the Giver of all things good for gifts that are simply too numerous to count.

MORE THOUGHTS ABOUT ATTITUDE

*The longer I live the more convinced I become
that life is 10 percent what happens to us
and 90 percent how we respond to it.*
CHARLES SWINDOLL

*We choose what attitudes we have right now.
And it's a continuing choice.*
JOHN MAXWELL

*Developing a positive attitude means working continually
to find what is uplifting and encouraging.*
BARBARA JOHNSON

*The things we think are the things
that feed our souls. If we think on pure
and lovely things, we shall grow pure and lovely
like them; and the converse is equally true.*
HANNAH WHITALL SMITH

*Those who are the happiest are not necessarily
those for whom life has been the easiest.
Emotional stability is an attitude.*
JAMES DOBSON

Each of us makes his own weather.
FULTON J. SHEEN

MORE FROM GOD'S WORD

A merry heart makes a cheerful countenance.
PROVERBS 15:13 NKJV

Rejoice always; pray without ceasing.
1 THESSALONIANS 5:16–17 NASB

Be glad and rejoice,
because your reward is great in heaven.
MATTHEW 5:12 HCSB

Finally, brothers, rejoice. Become mature,
be encouraged, be of the same mind, be at peace,
and the God of love and peace will be with you.
2 CORINTHIANS 13:11 HCSB

This is the day the LORD has made;
let us rejoice and be glad in it.
PSALM 118:24 HCSB

A TIMELY TIP

As a Christian, you have every reason on earth—and in heaven—to have a positive attitude. After all, God is in charge; He loves you; and He's prepared a place for you to live eternally with Him. To improve your attitude, focus more intently on the Lord's blessings and try to focus your thoughts on the positive aspects of life, not the negative ones. It is through gratitude, not grumpiness, that you will claim the best that life has to offer.

6

AVOIDING ARGUMENTS

AVOIDING DEAD-END ARGUMENTS

Avoiding a fight is a mark of honor;
only fools insist on quarreling.
PROVERBS 20:3 NLT

Time and again, God's Word warns us against angry outbursts and needless arguments. Arguments are seldom won but often lost, so when we acquire the unfortunate habit of habitual bickering, we do harm to our friends, to our families, to our coworkers, and to ourselves. When we engage in petty squabbles, our losses usually outpace our gains.

If you're dealing with a difficult person, you may be tempted to take the bait and argue over matters great and small. If you find yourself in that predicament, take a deep breath, say a silent prayer, and calm yourself down. Arguments are a monumental waste of time and energy. And since you're unlikely to win the argument anyway, there's no rational reason to participate.

Your words have echoes that extend beyond the here and now. So avoid anguished outpourings. Suppress your impulsive outbursts. Curb the need to criticize. Terminate tantrums. Learn to speak words that lift others up as you share a message of encouragement and hope with a world that needs both. When you talk, choose the very same words that you would use if Jesus were listening to your every word. Because He is.

MORE THOUGHTS ABOUT ARGUMENTS

*An argument seldom convinces anyone
contrary to his inclinations.*
THOMAS FULLER

*Whatever you do when conflicts arise, be wise.
Fight against jumping to quick conclusions
and seeing only your side. There are always
two sides on the streets of conflict. Look both ways.*
CHARLES SWINDOLL

Never persist in trying to set people right.
HANNAH WHITALL SMITH

Argument is the worst sort of conversation.
JONATHAN SWIFT

*Most serious conflicts evolve
from our attempts to control others
who will not accept our control.*
WILLIAM GLASSER

More from God's Word

People with quick tempers cause trouble,
but those who control their tempers stop a quarrel.
PROVERBS 15:18 NCV

If any man among you seem to be religious,
and bridleth not his tongue, but deceiveth
his own heart, this man's religion is vain.
JAMES 1:26 KJV

I tell you that on the day of judgment people
will have to account for every careless word they speak.
For by your words you will be acquitted,
and by your words you will be condemned.
MATTHEW 12:36–37 HCSB

A soft answer turneth away wrath:
but grievous words stir up anger.
PROVERBS 15:1 KJV

A Timely Tip

Arguments usually cause more problems than they solve. And if you're dealing with a highly emotional person, you probably won't win the argument anyway. So don't be afraid to leave the scene of an argument rather than engage in a debate that cannot be won. Dead-end arguments tend to increase stress and heighten anxiety, so you're better off avoiding them.

7

AVOIDING BURNOUT

AVOIDING BURNOUT

But those who wait on the LORD shall renew their strength;
they shall mount up with wings like eagles, they shall run
and not be weary, they shall walk and not faint.
ISAIAH 40:31 NKJV

Has the busy pace of life robbed you of the peace that might otherwise be yours through Jesus Christ? If so, you are simply too busy for your own good, and you're in danger of burning out.

Through His only begotten Son, God offers you a peace that passes human understanding, but He won't force His peace upon you. In order to experience it, you must slow down long enough to sense His presence and His love.

Time is a nonrenewable gift from above. How will you use it? You know from experience that you should invest some time each day in yourself, but finding time to do so is easier said than done. As a busy citizen of the twenty-first century, you may have difficulty investing large blocks of time in much-needed thought and self-reflection. If so, it may be time to reorder your priorities.

If you don't prioritize your day, other people will. Before you know it, you'll be taking on lots of new commitments, doing many things but few of them well. God, on the other hand, encourages you to slow down, to quiet yourself, and to spend time with Him. And you can be sure that God's way is best.

How will you organize your life? Will you carve out quiet moments with the Creator? And while you're at it, will you focus your energies and your resources on only the most important tasks on your to-do list? Will you summon the strength to say no when it's appropriate, or will you max out your schedule, leaving much of your most important work undone? Today, slow yourself down, commit more time to God, and spend less time on low-priority tasks. When you do, you'll be amazed at how the Father can revolutionize your life.

MORE THOUGHTS ABOUT AVOIDING BURNOUT

Life is strenuous. See that your clock does not run down.
LETTIE COWMAN

There are many burned-out people who think more is always better, who deem it unspiritual to say no.
SARAH YOUNG

Beware of having so much to do that you really do nothing at all because you do not wait upon God to do it aright.
C. H. SPURGEON

The sovereign cure for worry is prayer.
WILLIAM JAMES

MORE FROM GOD'S WORD

Don't burn out; keep yourselves fueled and aflame.
Be alert servants of the Master, cheerfully expectant.
Don't quit in hard times; pray all the harder.
ROMANS 12:11–12 MSG

Careful planning puts you ahead in the long run;
hurry and scurry puts you further behind.
PROVERBS 21:5 MSG

Abundant peace belongs to those who love
Your instruction; nothing makes them stumble.
PSALM 119:165 HCSB

But godliness with contentment is a great gain.
1 TIMOTHY 6:6 HCSB

I leave you peace; my peace I give you.
I do not give it to you as the world does.
So don't let your hearts be troubled or afraid.
JOHN 14:27 NCV

A TIMELY TIP

God can make all things new, including you. If you're feeling burned out or emotionally distraught, slow down, say a silent prayer, and focus on God's promises. And while you're at it, remember that Lord can renew your spirit and restore your strength. Your job, of course, is to let Him.

8

BIBLE STUDY

DIG DEEP INTO GOD'S WORD

*All Scripture is given by inspiration of God,
and is profitable for doctrine, for reproof,
for correction, for instruction in righteousness.*
2 TIMOTHY 3:16 KJV

If you're dealing with anxiety or fear, there's a book for that. It's called the Holy Bible. God's Word is unlike any other book. The words of Matthew 4:4 remind us, "Man shall not live by bread alone but by every word that proceedeth out of the mouth of God" (KJV).

As believers, we are instructed to study the Bible and meditate upon its meaning for our lives, yet far too many Bibles are laid aside by well-intentioned believers who would like to study the Bible if they could "just find the time."

Warren Wiersbe observed, "When the child of God looks into the Word of God, he sees the Son of God. And, he is transformed by the Spirit of God to share in the glory of God." God's holy Word is, indeed, a transforming, life-changing, one-of-a-kind treasure. And it's up to you—and only you—to use it that way.

MORE THOUGHTS ABOUT BIBLE STUDY

Do you want your faith to grow? Then let the Bible
begin to saturate your mind and soul.
BILLY GRAHAM

Gather the riches of God's promises.
Nobody can take away from you those texts
from the Bible which you have learned by heart.
CORRIE TEN BOOM

Read the scripture, not only as history,
but as a love letter sent to you from God.
THOMAS WATSON

I believe the reason so many are failing today is that they have
not disciplined themselves to read God's Word consistently, day
in and day out, and to apply it to every situation in life.
KAY ARTHUR

Reading the Bible has a purifying effect upon your life.
Let nothing take the place of this daily exercise.
BILLY GRAHAM

MORE FROM GOD'S WORD

The counsel of the LORD stands forever,
the plans of His heart from generation to generation.
PSALM 33:11 NASB

But grow in the grace and knowledge
of our Lord and Savior Jesus Christ.
To Him be the glory both now and to the day of eternity.
2 PETER 3:18 HCSB

You will be a good servant of Christ Jesus,
nourished by the words of the faith
and of the good teaching that you have followed.
1 TIMOTHY 4:6 HCSB

But the word of the Lord endures forever.
And this is the word that was preached as the gospel to you.
1 PETER 1:25 HCSB

But whoever looks intently into
the perfect law that gives freedom,
and continues in it—not forgetting what
they have heard, but doing it—
they will be blessed in what they do.
JAMES 1:25 NIV

A TIMELY TIP

The Bible is God's guidebook for every situation you'll ever face, and it's the perfect book to help you manage your anxieties and fears. Even if you've studied the Bible for many years, you've still got lots to learn. Bible study should be a lifelong endeavor. Make it *your* lifelong endeavor.

9

BLESSINGS

FOCUS ON BLESSINGS, NOT BURDENS

Blessings crown the head of the righteous.
PROVERBS 10:6 NIV

When you're feeling anxious or fearful, it's easy to focus on your problems, not your blessings. A far better strategy, of course, is to focus on your blessings, not your burdens.

If you tried to count all your blessings, how long would it take? A very, very long time. After all, you've been given the priceless gift of life here on earth and the promise of life eternal in heaven. And you've been given so much more.

Billy Graham noted: "We should think of the blessings we so easily take for granted: Life itself; preservation from danger; every bit of health we enjoy; every hour of liberty; the ability to see, to hear, to speak, to think, and to imagine all this comes from the hand of God." That's sound advice for believers—followers of the One from Galilee—who have so much to be thankful for.

Your blessings, all of which are gifts from above, are indeed too numerous to count, but it never hurts to begin counting them anyway. Even when times are tough, it's always the right time to say thanks to the Giver for the gifts you can count, and all the other ones too.

More Thoughts about God's Blessings

We do not need to beg Him to bless us;
He simply cannot help it.
HANNAH WHITALL SMITH

God is always trying to give good things to us,
but our hands are too full to receive them.
ST. AUGUSTINE

God's gifts put man's best dreams to shame.
ELIZABETH BARRETT BROWNING

God is the giver, and we are the receivers.
And His richest gifts are bestowed not upon
those who do the greatest things, but upon those
who accept His abundance and His grace.
HANNAH WHITALL SMITH

God has promised us abundance, peace,
and eternal life. These treasures are ours
for the asking. One of the great mysteries
of life is why so many of us wait so long
to lay claim to God's gifts.
MARIE T. FREEMAN

More from God's Word

The Lord is my rock, my fortress, and my deliverer, my God,
my mountain where I seek refuge. My shield, the horn of my
salvation, my stronghold, my refuge, and my Savior.
2 Samuel 22:2–3 HCSB

May Yahweh bless you and protect you;
may Yahweh make His face shine on you and be gracious to you.
Numbers 6:24–25 HCSB

You will show me the path of life; in Your presence is fullness
of joy; at Your right hand are pleasures forevermore.
Psalm 16:11 NKJV

The Lord is good to all: and his
tender mercies are over all his works.
Psalm 145:9 KJV

The Lord is my shepherd; I shall not want.
Psalm 23:1 KJV

A Timely Tip

When you're feeling anxious or afraid, remind yourself that you are
still richly blessed. In truth, God has given you more blessings than
you can possibly count, but it doesn't hurt to begin counting them.
And while you're at it, don't forget to praise the Giver of all those
incalculable gifts.

10

CELEBRATION

THE TIME TO CELEBRATE IS NOW

Rejoice always, pray without ceasing, in everything give thanks; for this is the will of God in Christ Jesus for you.
1 THESSALONIANS 5:16–18 NKJV

Today is a nonrenewable resource—once it's gone, it's gone forever. Our responsibility, as thoughtful believers, is to use this day in the service of God's will and in the service of His people. When we do so, we enrich our own lives and the lives of those whom we love.

God has richly blessed us, and He wants you to rejoice in His gifts. That's why this day—and each day that follows—should be a time of prayer and celebration as we consider the Good News of God's free gift: the gift of eternal life through Jesus Christ.

Oswald Chambers correctly observed, "Joy is the great note all throughout the Bible." E. Stanley Jones echoed that thought when he wrote, "Christ and joy go together." But even the most dedicated believers can, on occasion, forget to celebrate each day for what it is: a priceless gift from God.

What do you expect from the day ahead? Are you expecting the Lord to do wonderful things, or are you living beneath a cloud of apprehension and doubt? Today, celebrate the life that God has given you. Today, put a smile on your face, kind words on your lips, and a song in your heart. Be generous with your praise and free with your encouragement. And then, when you have celebrated life to the full, invite your friends to do likewise. After all, this is God's day, and He has given us clear instructions for its use. We are commanded to rejoice and be glad. So with no further ado, let the celebration begin . . .

MORE THOUGHTS ABOUT CELEBRATING LIFE

All our life is celebration to us. We are convinced, in fact, that God is always everywhere.
ST. CLEMENT OF ALEXANDRIA

The greatest honor you can give Almighty God is to live gladly and joyfully because of the knowledge of His love.
JULIAN OF NORWICH

Every day we live is a priceless gift of God, loaded with possibilities to learn something new, to gain fresh insights.
DALE EVANS ROGERS

Joy is the direct result of having God's perspective on our daily lives and the effect of loving our Lord enough to obey His commands and trust His promises.
BILL BRIGHT

*There is not one blade of grass, there is no color
in this world that is not intended to make us rejoice.*
JOHN CALVIN

MORE FROM GOD'S WORD

I delight greatly in the LORD; my soul rejoices in my God.
ISAIAH 61:10 NIV

I came that they may have life, and have it abundantly.
JOHN 10:10 NASB

A happy heart is like a continual feast.
PROVERBS 15:15 NCV

*This is the day which the LORD has made;
let us rejoice and be glad in it.*
PSALM 118:24 NASB

Rejoice in the Lord always. Again I will say, rejoice!
PHILIPPIANS 4:4 NKJV

A TIMELY TIP

When times are tough and you're feeling anxious or afraid, it's easy to become discouraged. Easy, but wrong. Even during your darkest days, you still have many reasons to celebrate. So focus on the positive aspects of life and count your blessings, not your hardships. Don't let your emotions be hijacked by momentary hardships. Focus, instead, on God's never-ending love.

11

CHRIST'S LOVE

EXPERIENCING CHRIST'S LOVE AND SHARING IT

We love him, because he first loved us.
1 JOHN 4:19 KJV

Hannah Whitall Smith spoke to believers of every generation when she advised, "Keep your face upturned to Christ as the flowers do to the sun. Look, and your soul shall live and grow." But when we're dealing with difficult people, it becomes harder to focus on Christ's love because we are overwhelmed by other emotions. It's hard to focus on Jesus, but not impossible. When we turn our hearts to Him we receive His blessings, His peace, and His grace.

Christ is the ultimate Savior of mankind and the personal Savior of those who believe in Him. As His servants, we should place Him at the very center of our lives. And every day that God gives us breath, we should share Christ's love and His message with a world that needs both.

Christ's love changes everything, including you. When you accept His gift of grace, you are transformed, not only for the moment, but also for all eternity. He's waiting patiently for you to invite Him into your heart. Please don't make Him wait a single minute longer.

MORE THOUGHTS ABOUT CHRIST'S LOVE

*Above all else, the Christian life
is a love affair of the heart.*
JOHN ELDREDGE

Jesus: the proof of God's love.
PHILLIP YANCEY

*Jesus is all compassion.
He never betrays us.*
CATHERINE MARSHALL

*As the love of a husband for his bride,
such is the love of Christ for His people.*
C. H. SPURGEON

*The love of God exists in
its strongest and purest form
in the very midst of suffering and tragedy.*
SUZANNE DALE EZELL

MORE FROM GOD'S WORD

As the Father loved Me, I also
have loved you; abide in My love.
JOHN 15:9 NKJV

For Christ also suffered once for sins, the just
for the unjust, that He might bring us to God, being
put to death in the flesh but made alive by the Spirit.
1 PETER 3:18 NKJV

I am the good shepherd. The good shepherd
lays down his life for the sheep.
JOHN 10:11 HCSB

No one has greater love than this, that someone
would lay down his life for his friends.
JOHN 15:13 HCSB

For God so loved the world, that he gave his
only begotten Son, that whosoever believeth in him
should not perish, but have everlasting life.
JOHN 3:16 KJV

A TIMELY TIP

Christ's love is meant to be experienced—and shared—by you. If you're feeling anxious or afraid, it's time to remind yourself that your problems are temporary but Christ's love lasts forever.

12

CHURCH

GET INVOLVED IN YOUR CHURCH

Be on guard for yourselves and for all the flock that the Holy Spirit has appointed you to as overseers, to shepherd the church of God, which He purchased with His own blood.
ACTS 20:28 HCSB

The Bible teaches that we should worship God in our hearts and in our churches (Acts 20:28). We have clear instructions to "feed the church of God" and to worship our Creator in the presence of fellow believers.

We live in a world that is teeming with temptations, distractions, and fear-provoking situations—a world where good and evil struggle in a constant battle to win our minds, our hearts, and our souls. Our challenge, of course, is to ensure that we cast our lot on the side of God. One way that we remain faithful to Him is through the practice of regular, purposeful worship. When we worship the Father faithfully and fervently, we are blessed.

Fellowship with other believers should be an integral part of your everyday life. Your association with fellow Christians should be uplifting, enlightening, encouraging, and consistent.

Are you an active member of your own fellowship? Are you a builder of bridges inside the four walls of your church and outside it? Do you contribute to God's glory by contributing your time and your talents to a close-knit band of believers? Hopefully so. The fellowship of believers is intended to be a powerful tool for spreading God's Good News and uplifting His children. And God intends for you to be a fully contributing member of that fellowship. Your intentions should be the same.

MORE THOUGHTS ABOUT CHURCH

Every believer is commanded to be plugged in to a local church.
DAVID JEREMIAH

Churchgoers are like coals in a fire. When they cling together, they keep the flame aglow; when they separate, they die out.
BILLY GRAHAM

The church is a hospital for sinners, not a museum for saints.
VANCE HAVNER

The Church will outlive the universe; in it the individual person will outlive the universe.
C. S. LEWIS

Divisions between Christians are a sin and a scandal, and Christians ought at all times to be making contributions toward reunion, if it is only by their prayers.

More from God's Word

I was glad when they said unto me,
Let us go into the house of the LORD.
PSALM 122:1 KJV

God is spirit, and those who worship Him
must worship in spirit and truth.
JOHN 4:24 HCSB

For where two or three come together in my name,
there am I with them.
MATTHEW 18:20 NIV

Enter his gates with thanksgiving, go into his courts
with praise. Give thanks to him and bless his name.
PSALM 100:4 NLT

Worship the Lord your God, and serve only Him.
MATTHEW 4:10 HCSB

A Timely Tip

What you put into church determines what you get out of it. Your attitude towards worship is vitally important to your spiritual and emotional health, so attend church regularly and celebrate accordingly.

13

CONFIDENCE

DRAW CONFIDENCE FROM GOD

*Let us hold tightly without wavering to the hope
we affirm, for God can be trusted to keep his promise.*
HEBREWS 10:23 NLT

Are you confident about your future, or do you live under a cloud of anxiety and doubt? If you trust God's promises, you have every reason to live comfortably and confidently. But despite God's promises, and despite His blessings, you may, from time to time, find yourself being tormented by negativity and fear. If so, it's time to redirect your thoughts and your prayers.

Even the most optimistic men and women may be overcome by occasional bouts of fear and anxiety. You are no different. But even when you feel discouraged—or worse—you should remember that God is always faithful, and you are always protected.

Every life, including yours, is a series of successes and failures, celebrations and disappointments, joys and sorrows, hopes and doubts. But even when you feel very distant from God, remember that He is never distant from you. When you sincerely seek His presence, He will touch your heart, calm your fears, and restore your confidence. No challenge is too big for Him. Not even yours.

More Thoughts about Confidence

Never yield to gloomy anticipation.
Place your hope and confidence in God.
He has no record of failure.
LETTIE COWMAN

One of the marks of spiritual maturity
is the quiet confidence that God is in control,
without the need to understand
why He does what He does.
CHARLES SWINDOLL

When a train goes through a tunnel
and it gets dark, you don't throw away your ticket
and jump off. You sit still and trust the engineer.
CORRIE TEN BOOM

Faith and obedience are bound up
in the same bundle. He that obeys God,
trusts God; and he that trusts God, obeys God.
C. H. SPURGEON

Confidence imparts a wonderful
inspiration to its possessor.
JOHN MILTON

Never be afraid to trust an unknown future to a known God.
CORRIE TEN BOOM

More from God's Word

Let us draw near with a true heart in full assurance of faith,
our hearts sprinkled clean from an evil conscience and our
bodies washed in pure water.
HEBREWS 10:22 HCSB

In quietness and in confidence shall be your strength.
ISAIAH 30:15 KJV

For our gospel came not unto you in word only, but also in
power, and in the Holy Ghost, and in much assurance.
1 THESSALONIANS 1:5 KJV

As for God, his way is perfect: the word of the LORD is tried:
he is a buckler to all those that trust in him.
PSALM 18:30 KJV

And this is the secret: Christ lives in you.
This gives you assurance of sharing his glory.
COLOSSIANS 1:27 NLT

A Timely Tip

If negative emotions have caused you to doubt your abilities or your opportunities, it's time for a complete mental makeover. God created you for a purpose, and He has important work specifically for you. So don't let anxious feelings or irrational fears steal your joy, your self-confidence, or your faith in God. Because the Lord is faithful, you can be confident that you are protected and your future is secure.

14

COURAGE

WHEN YOUR HEART IS TROUBLED, TAKE COURAGE

*For God has not given us a spirit of fearfulness,
but one of power, love, and sound judgment.*
2 TIMOTHY 1:7 HCSB

Every person's life is a tapestry of events: some wonderful, some not-so-wonderful, and some downright disastrous. When we visit the mountaintops of life, praising God isn't hard; in fact, it's easy. In our moments of triumph, we can bow our heads and thank God for our victories. But when we fail to reach the mountaintops, when we endure the inevitable losses that are a part of every person's life, we find it much tougher to give God the praise He deserves. Yet wherever we find ourselves, whether on the mountaintops of life or in life's darkest valleys, we must still offer thanks to God, giving thanks in all circumstances.

God is not a distant being. He is not absent from our world, nor is He absent from your world. God is not "out there"; He is "right here," continuously reshaping His universe, and continuously reshaping the lives of those who dwell in it.

The Lord is with you always, listening to your thoughts and

prayers, watching over your every move. If the demands of everyday life weigh down upon you, you may be tempted to ignore God's presence or—worse yet—to lose faith in His promises. But when you quiet yourself and acknowledge His presence, God will touch your heart and restore your courage.

MORE THOUGHTS ABOUT COURAGE

Courage is not simply one of the virtues,
but the form of every virtue at the testing point.
C. S. LEWIS

Action springs not from thought,
but from a readiness for responsibility.
DIETRICH BONHOEFFER

In my experience, God rarely makes our fear disappear.
Instead, He asks us to be strong and take courage.
BRUCE WILKINSON

Just as courage is faith in good, so discouragement
is faith in evil, and, while courage opens the door to good,
discouragement opens it to evil.
HANNAH WHITALL SMITH

Fill your mind with thoughts of God
rather than with thoughts of fear.
NORMAN VINCENT PEALE

Do not limit the limitless God! With Him,
face the future unafraid because you are never alone.
LETTIE COWMAN

MORE FROM GOD'S WORD

But He said to them, "It is I; do not be afraid."
JOHN 6:20 NKJV

Behold, God is my salvation; I will trust, and not be afraid.
ISAIAH 12:2 KJV

Be on guard. Stand firm in the faith.
Be courageous. Be strong.
1 CORINTHIANS 16:13 NLT

I can do all things through Him who strengthens me.
PHILIPPIANS 4:13 NASB

Be strong and courageous, and do the work. Do not be afraid
or discouraged, for the LORD God, my God, is with you.
1 CHRONICLES 28:20 NIV

A TIMELY TIP

It takes insight and courage to deal effectively with negative emotions. If you need insight, talk to people you trust and spend time studying God's Word. And if you need courage, ask the Lord to help you do what needs to be done. Now.

15

DAILY DEVOTIONAL

START EVERY DAY WITH GOD

*Morning by morning he wakens me
and opens my understanding to his will.
The Sovereign LORD has spoken to me, and I have listened.*
ISAIAH 50:4–5 NLT

A great way to prepare yourself for the rigors of everyday living is by spending a few moments with God every morning. Whether you're dealing with roller-coaster emotions, stressful circumstances, or exaggerated fears, you need God as your partner. So if you find that you're simply "too busy" for a daily chat with your Father in heaven, it's time to take a long, hard look at your priorities and your values.

Each day has 1,440 minutes. Do you value your relationship with God enough to spend a few of those minutes with Him? He deserves that much of your time and more. Is He receiving it from you? Hopefully so.

As you consider your plans for the day ahead, here's a tip: Organize your life around this simple principle: "God first." When you place your Creator where He belongs—at the very center of your day and your life—the rest of your priorities will fall into place.

More Thoughts about Your Daily Devotional

Whatever is your best time in the day,
give that to communion with God.
Hudson Taylor

Begin each day with God.
It will change your priorities.
Elizabeth George

Relying on God has to begin all over again
every day as if nothing had yet been done.
C. S. Lewis

The entire day receives order and discipline
when it acquires unity. This unity
must be sought and found in morning prayer.
The morning prayer determines the day.
Dietrich Bonhoeffer

Make it the first morning business of your life
to understand some part of the Bible clearly,
and make it your daily business to obey it.
John Ruskin

Doesn't God deserve the best minutes of your day?
Billy Graham

More from God's Word

Early the next morning, while it was still dark,
Jesus woke and left the house.
He went to a lonely place, where he prayed.
MARK 1:35 NCV

But grow in the grace and knowledge
of our Lord and Savior Jesus Christ.
To Him be the glory both now and to the day of eternity.
2 PETER 3:18 HCSB

Heaven and earth will pass away,
but My words will never pass away.
MATTHEW 24:35 HCSB

Thy word is a lamp unto my feet,
and a light unto my path.
PSALM 119:105 KJV

It is good to give thanks to the LORD,
and to sing praises to Your name, O Most High.
PSALM 92:1 NKJV

A Timely Tip

A regular time of quiet reflection, prayer, and Bible study will allow you to praise your Creator, to focus your thoughts, and to seek God's guidance on matters great and small. Don't miss this opportunity.

16

DEALING WITH ADVERSITY

TOUGH TIMES NEVER LAST, TOUGH PEOPLE DO

God blesses those who patiently endure testing and temptation.
Afterward they will receive the crown of life
that God has promised to those who love him.
JAMES 1:12 NLT

The times that try men's and women's souls are also the times when character is forged on the anvil of adversity. But the character building is never easy. Overcoming tough times requires strength, prayer, insight, and perseverance.

During difficult times, we are tempted to complain, to worry, to blame other people, and to do little else. Usually complaints and worries change nothing; intelligent action, on the other hand, can change everything.

If you find yourself enduring difficult circumstances—or if you're paralyzed by doubts about your faith or your future—remember that God remains in His heaven. He is a God of possibility, not negativity.

So the next time you feel anxious, or fearful, or worried, turn those negative emotions over to God. He will guide you through your difficulties and beyond them. And then, with a renewed spirit of optimism and hope, you can thank the Giver of all things good for gifts that are too profound to fully comprehend and too numerous to count.

MORE THOUGHTS ABOUT DEALING WITH ADVERSITY

God is in control. He may not take away trials or make detours for us, but He strengthens us through them.
BILLY GRAHAM

God alone can give us songs in the night.
C. H. SPURGEON

Often God has to shut a door in our face so that he can subsequently open the door through which He wants us to go.
CATHERINE MARSHALL

Human problems are never greater than divine solutions.
ERWIN LUTZER

Life is literally filled with God-appointed storms. These squalls surge across everyone's horizon. We all need them.
CHARLES SWINDOLL

More from God's Word

He heals the brokenhearted and binds up their wounds.
PSALM 147:3 HCSB

I called to the LORD in my distress;
I called to my God. From His temple He heard my voice.
2 SAMUEL 22:7 HCSB

We are hard-pressed on every side,
yet not crushed; we are perplexed,
but not in despair.
2 CORINTHIANS 4:8 NKJV

The LORD is my rock, my fortress, and my deliverer,
my God, my mountain where I seek refuge.
My shield, the horn of my salvation,
my stronghold, my refuge, and my Savior.
2 SAMUEL 22:2–3 HCSB

The LORD is my shepherd; I shall not want.
PSALM 23:1 KJV

A Timely Tip

Perhaps, because of tough times, you're being forced to step outside your comfort zone. If so, consider it an opportunity to grow spiritually and emotionally. Your challenge is to trust yourself, to trust God, and to follow His lead.

17

DEALING WITH CHANGE
DEALING WITH CONSTANT CHANGE

*To every thing there is a season,
and a time to every purpose under the heaven.*
ECCLESIASTES 3:1 KJV

Our world is in a state of constant change. God is not. At times
the world seems to be trembling beneath our feet. But we can be
comforted in the knowledge that our heavenly Father is the rock
that cannot be shaken.

Every day that we live, we mortals encounter a multitude of
changes—some good, some not so good. And on occasion all of us
must endure life-changing personal losses that leave us heartbroken.
When we do, our heavenly Father stands ready to comfort us, to
guide us, and—in time—to heal us.

Is the world spinning a little too fast for your liking? Are you
facing difficult circumstances or unwelcome changes? If so, please
remember that God is far bigger than any problem you may face. So
instead of worrying about life's inevitable challenges, put your faith
in the Father and His only begotten Son. After all, "Jesus Christ is
the same yesterday, today, and forever" (Hebrews 13:8 NKJV). And
it is precisely because your Savior does not change that you can face

your challenges with courage for today and hope for tomorrow.

Are you anxious about situations that you cannot control? Take your anxieties to God. Are you troubled? Take your troubles to Him. Does your little corner of the universe seem to be trembling beneath your feet? Seek protection from the One who cannot be moved. The same God who created the universe will protect you if you ask Him, so ask Him . . . and then serve Him with willing hands and a trusting heart.

DEALING WITH CHANGE

Are you on the eve of change? Embrace it. Accept it.
Don't resist it. Change is not only a part of life,
change is a necessary part of God's strategy.
To use us to change the world, He alters our assignments.
MAX LUCADO

Transitions are almost always signs of growth,
but they can bring feelings of loss. To get somewhere new,
we may have to leave somewhere else behind.
FRED ROGERS

Change the fabric of your own soul and your
own visions, and you change all.
VACHEL LINDSAY

The world changes—circumstances change,
we change—but God's Word never changes.
WARREN WIERSBE

More from God's Word

I am the LORD, and I do not change.
MALACHI 3:6 NLT

*But grow in the grace and knowledge
of our Lord and Savior Jesus Christ.
To Him be the glory both now and forever. Amen.*
2 PETER 3:18 NKJV

*Then He who sat on the throne said,
"Behold, I make all things new."*
REVELATION 21:5 NKJV

*When I was a child, I spoke like a child,
I thought like a child, I reasoned like a child.
When I became a man, I put aside childish things.*
1 CORINTHIANS 13:11 HCSB

*The wise see danger ahead and avoid it, b
ut fools keep going and get into trouble.*
PROVERBS 22:3 NCV

A Timely Tip

Change is inevitable; growth is not. God will come to your doorstep on countless occasions with opportunities to learn and to grow. And He will knock. Your challenge, of course, is to open the door.

18

DEALING WITH DIFFICULT PEOPLE

WHEN DIFFICULT PEOPLE THREATEN TO HIJACK YOUR EMOTIONS

Bad temper is contagious—don't get infected.
PROVERBS 22:25 MSG

Sometimes people can be cruel, discourteous, untruthful, or rude. When other people do or say things that are hurtful, you may become anxious or angry. So you may be tempted to strike back with a verbal salvo of your own. But before you say words that can never be unsaid, slow down, say a quiet prayer, and remember this: God corrects other people's behaviors in His own way, and He doesn't need your help (even if you're totally convinced you're in the right).

The Bible teaches us to be self-controlled, thoughtful, and mature. But the world often tempts us to behave otherwise. Everywhere we turn, or so it seems, we see undisciplined, unruly role models who behave impulsively yet experience few, if any, negative consequences. So it's not surprising that when we meet folks whose personalities conflict with our own, we're tempted to respond in undisciplined, unruly ways. But there's a catch: if we fall prey to immaturity or impulsivity, those behaviors inevitably cause more problems than they solve.

So when other people behave cruelly, foolishly, or impulsively, as they will from time to time, don't allow yourself to become caught up in their emotional distress. Instead, speak up for yourself as politely as you can and, if necessary, walk away. Next, forgive everybody as quickly as you can. Then get on with your life, and leave the rest up to God.

MORE THOUGHTS ABOUT DEALING WITH DIFFICULT PEOPLE

Whatever a person may be like,
we must still love them because we love God.
JOHN CALVIN

How often should you forgive the other person?
Only as many times as you want God to forgive you!
MARIE T. FREEMAN

Never allow sick attitudes to poison your thinking,
nor let ill will make you ill.
NORMAN VINCENT PEALE

If you are having difficulty loving or relating to an individual,
take him to God. Bother the Lord with this person. Don't you
be bothered with him—leave him at the throne.
CHARLES SWINDOLL

More from God's Word

Mockers can get a whole town agitated,
but the wise will calm anger.
PROVERBS 29:8 NLT

Stay away from a foolish man;
you will gain no knowledge from his speech.
PROVERBS 14:7 HCSB

Don't make friends with an angry man,
and don't be a companion of a hot-tempered man,
or you will learn his ways and entangle yourself in a snare.
PROVERBS 22:24–25 HCSB

A person with great anger bears the penalty;
if you rescue him, you'll have to do it again.
PROVERBS 19:19 HCSB

A perverse person stirs up conflict,
and a gossip separates close friends.
PROVERBS 16:28 NIV

A Timely Tip

Pick your friends wisely. If you want to maintain a positive attitude, it's important to associate with people who are upbeat, optimistic, and encouraging. Sometimes misguided people may attempt to alleviate their own pain by inflicting pain upon others. If you find yourself caught up in a relationship that is detrimental to your spiritual or emotional health, give yourself permission to walk away.

19

DEALING WITH FAILURE

EXPERIENCING SETBACKS
AND STAYING ON COURSE

For though the righteous fall seven times, they rise again.
PROVERBS 24:16 NIV

If you want to combat negative emotions like anxiety and fear, you must learn how to deal with failure. Why? Because all of us face setbacks from time to time. We all experience occasional disappointments that are simply the price we pay for being dues-paying members of the human race.

Hebrews 10:36 advises, "Patient endurance is what you need now, so that you will continue to do God's will. Then you will receive all that he has promised" (NLT). These words remind us that when we persevere, we will eventually receive the rewards that God has promised us. What's required is perseverance, not perfection.

When we face hardships, God stands ready to protect us. Our responsibility, of course, is to ask Him for protection. When we call upon Him in heartfelt prayer, He will answer—in His own time and according to His own plan—and He will do His part to heal us. We, of course, must do our part too. And while we are waiting for God's plans to unfold and for His healing touch to restore us, we can be comforted in the knowledge that our Creator can overcome any obstacle, even if we cannot.

MORE THOUGHTS ABOUT DEALING WITH FAILURE

No amount of falls will really undo us
if we keep picking ourselves up after each one.
C. S. LEWIS

No matter how badly we have failed, we can always get up
and begin again. Our God is the God of new beginnings.
WARREN WIERSBE

Mistakes offer the possibility for redemption
and a new start in God's kingdom. No matter what
you're guilty of, God can restore your innocence.
BARBARA JOHNSON

Every calamity is a spur and valuable hint.
RALPH WALDO EMERSON

Those who have failed miserably are often
the first to see God's formula for success.
ERWIN LUTZER

Failure is one of life's most powerful teachers.
How we handle our failures determines whether
we're going to simply "get by" in life or "press on."
BETH MOORE

More from God's Word

Weeping may endure for a night,
but joy comes in the morning.
PSALM 30:5 NKJV

If you listen to correction to improve your life,
you will live among the wise.
PROVERBS 15:31 NCV

But as for you, be strong; don't be discouraged,
for your work has a reward.
2 CHRONICLES 15:7 HCSB

We are hard-pressed on every side, yet not crushed;
we are perplexed, but not in despair.
2 CORINTHIANS 4:8 NKJV

The LORD is near to those who have a broken heart.
PSALM 34:18 NKJV

A Timely Tip

Setbacks are inevitable, but your response to them is optional. You and the Lord, working together, can always find a way to turn stumbling blocks into stepping stones, so don't give up, don't abandon hope, and don't be afraid. Better days will arrive, and perhaps sooner than you think.

20

DEPRESSION

UNDERSTANDING DEPRESSION

He heals the brokenhearted and binds up their wounds.
PSALM 147:3 HCSB

It has been said, and with good reason, that depression is the common cold of mental illness. Why? Because depression is such a common malady. But make no mistake: depression is a serious condition that, if untreated, can take a terrible toll on individuals and families alike.

The sadness that accompanies any significant loss is an inescapable fact of life. Throughout our lives, all of us must endure the kinds of deep personal losses that leave us struggling to find hope. But in time, we move beyond our grief as the sadness runs its course and gradually abates. Depression, on the other hand, is a physical and emotional condition that is, in almost all cases, treatable with medication and counseling. Depression is not a disease to be taken lightly. Left untreated, it presents real dangers to patients' physical health and to their emotional well-being.

If you find yourself feeling "blue," perhaps it's a logical reaction to the ups and downs of daily life. But if your feelings of sadness have lasted longer than you think they should—or if someone close to you fears that your sadness may have evolved into clinical depression—it's time to seek professional help.

Here are a few simple guidelines to consider as you make decisions about possible medical treatment:

- If you have persistent urges toward self-destructive behavior, or if you feel as though you have lost the will to live, consult a professional counselor or physician immediately.
- If someone you trust urges you to seek counseling, schedule a session with a professionally trained counselor to evaluate your condition.
- If you experience persistent and prolonged changes in sleep patterns, or if you experience a significant change in weight (either gain or loss), consult your physician.
- If you are plagued by consistent, prolonged, severe feelings of hopelessness, consult a physician, a professional counselor, or your pastor.

In the familiar words of John 10:10, Jesus promises, "I have come that they may have life, and that they may have it more abundantly" (NKJV). And in John 15:11 He states, "These things I have spoken to you, that My joy may remain in you, and that your joy may be full." These two passages make it clear: our Lord intends that we experience lives of joyful abundance through Him. Our duty, as grateful believers, is to do everything we can to receive the joy and abundance that can be ours in Christ—and the term "everything" includes appropriate medical treatment when necessary.

Some days are light and happy, and some days are not. When we face the inevitable dark days of life, we must choose how we will respond. Will we allow ourselves to sink even more deeply into our own sadness, or will we do the difficult work of pulling ourselves out? We bring light to the dark days of life by turning first to God, and then to trusted family members, to friends, and, in some cases, to medical professionals. When we do, the clouds will eventually part, and the sun will shine once more upon our souls.

MORE THOUGHTS ABOUT DEPRESSION

Perhaps the greatest psychological,
spiritual, and medical need that
all people have is the need for hope.
BILLY GRAHAM

Emotions we have not poured out
in the safe hands of God can turn into feelings
of hopelessness and depression. God is safe.
BETH MOORE

I am sure it is never sadness—a proper, straight,
natural response to loss—that does people harm,
but all the other things, all the resentment, dismay, doubt,
and self-pity with which it is usually complicated.
C. S. LEWIS

Feelings of uselessness and hopelessness
are not from God, but from the evil one,
the devil, who wants to discourage you
and thwart your effectiveness for the Lord.
BILL BRIGHT

MORE FROM GOD'S WORD

Your heart must not be troubled.
Believe in God; believe also in Me.
JOHN 14:1 HCSB

When I sit in darkness, the LORD will be a light to me.
MICAH 7:8 NKJV

Weeping may endure for a night,
but joy comes in the morning.
PSALM 30:5 NKJV

Blessed are the poor in spirit: for theirs
is the kingdom of heaven. Blessed are they
that mourn: for they shall be comforted.
MATTHEW 5:3–4 KJV

Why are you cast down, O my soul? And why
are you disquieted within me? Hope in God;
for I shall yet praise Him, the help
of my countenance and my God.
PSALM 42:11 NKJV

A TIMELY TIP

If you're feeling very sad or deeply depressed, talk about it with people who can help. Don't hesitate to speak with your doctor or your pastor or both. Help is available. Ask for it.

21

DIET AND EXERCISE

Therefore, I urge you, brothers and sisters, in view of God's mercy, to offer your bodies as a living sacrifice, holy and pleasing to God—this is your true and proper worship.
ROMANS 12:1 NIV

In the book of Romans, Paul encourages us to make our bodies "holy and pleasing to God." Paul adds that to do so is "true and proper worship." For believers, the implication is clear: God intends that we take special care of the bodies He has given us. But it's tempting to do otherwise.

We live in a fast-food world where unhealthy choices are convenient, inexpensive, and tempting. And we live in a digital world filled with modern conveniences that often rob us of the physical exercise needed to maintain healthy lifestyles. As a result, too many of us find ourselves glued to the television, with a snack in one hand and a clicker in the other. The results are as unfortunate as they are predictable.

As adults, each of us bears a personal responsibility for the general state of our own physical health. Certainly, various aspects of health are beyond our control: illness sometimes strikes even the healthiest men and women. But for most of us, physical health is a choice: it is the result of hundreds of small decisions that we make every day of our lives. If we make decisions that promote good health, our bodies respond. But if we fall into bad habits and undisciplined lifestyles, we can inadvertently cause ourselves significant harm.

When you combine sensible exercise with a nutritious diet, you'll feel better and you'll discover the stress-reducing effects of a healthy lifestyle. So if you're being victimized by your own unhealthy habits, today is the perfect day for a change. You can start by taking personal responsibility for the body that God has given you. Then, make the solemn pledge to yourself that you will begin to make the changes that are required to enjoy a longer, healthier, happier life. No one can make those changes for you; you must make them for yourself. And with God's help, you can do it. With Him, all things are possible.

MORE THOUGHTS ABOUT TAKING CARE OF YOUR BODY

Discipline, for the Christian, begins with the body. We have only one. It is this body that is the primary material given to us for sacrifice. We cannot give our hearts to God and keep our bodies for ourselves.
ELISABETH ELLIOT

God wants you to give Him your body. Some people do foolish things with their bodies. God wants your body as a holy sacrifice.
WARREN WIERSBE

Our body is a portable sanctuary through which we are daily experiencing the presence of God.
RICHARD FOSTER

More from God's Word

So whether you eat or drink, or whatever you do,
do it all for the glory of God.
1 Corinthians 10:31 NLT

You should know that your body is a temple for
the Holy Spirit who is in you. You have received
the Holy Spirit from God. So you do not belong
to yourselves, because you were bought by God
for a price. So honor God with your bodies.
1 Corinthians 6:19–20 NCV

You made all the delicate, inner parts
of my body and knit me together
in my mother's womb. Thank you for
making me so wonderfully complex! Your workmanship
is marvelous—and how well I know it.
Psalm 139:13–14 NLT

Yet you made them only a little lower than God,
and crowned them with glory and honor.
Psalm 8:5 NLT

A Timely Tip

If you feel the need to improve your physical health, don't wait for New Year's Day; don't even wait until tomorrow. When it comes to the important business of improving your physical health, the time to get started is now. Later may be too late.

22

DIFFICULT CIRCUMSTANCES

TRUST HIM IN EVERY CIRCUMSTANCE

Trust in him at all times, you people;
pour out your hearts to him, for God is our refuge.
PSALM 62:8 NIV

Every human life (including yours) is a tapestry of events: some grand, some not-so-grand, and some downright disheartening. When we reach the mountaintops of life, praising God is easy. But when the storm clouds form overhead and we find ourselves in the dark valley of despair, our faith is stretched, sometimes to the breaking point. As Christians, we can be comforted: wherever we find ourselves, whether at the top of the mountain or the depths of the valley, God is there, and because He cares for us, we can live courageously.

The Bible promises this: tough times are temporary but God's love is not—God's love lasts forever. So what does that mean to you? Just this: from time to time, everybody faces tough times, and so will you. When those tough times arrive, you need not be afraid because God always stands ready to protect you and heal you.

Psalm 147 promises, "He heals the brokenhearted" (v. 3 NIV), but it doesn't say that His healing is instantaneous. Usually it takes time (and maybe even a little help from you) for God to fix things. So if you're facing tough times, face them with God by your side. If you find yourself in any kind of trouble, pray about it and ask God for help. And be patient. God will work things out, just as He has promised, but He will do it in His own way and in His own time.

MORE THOUGHTS ABOUT TRUSTING GOD IN DIFFICULT CIRCUMSTANCES

Jesus did not promise to change the circumstances around us. He promised great peace and pure joy to those who would learn to believe that God actually controls all things.
CORRIE TEN BOOM

Don't let obstacles along the road to eternity shake your confidence in God's promises.
DAVID JEREMIAH

No time is too hard for God, no situation too difficult.
NORMAN VINCENT PEALE

Accept each day as it comes to you. Do not waste your time and energy wishing for a different set of circumstances.
SARAH YOUNG

Every experience God gives us, every person He brings into our lives, is the perfect preparation for the future that only He can see.
CORRIE TEN BOOM

No matter what our circumstance,
we can find a reason to be thankful.

DAVID JEREMIAH

MORE FROM GOD'S WORD

Cast your burden on the LORD, and He shall sustain you;
He shall never permit the righteous to be moved.
PSALM 55:22 NKJV

The LORD is a refuge for the oppressed,
a refuge in times of trouble.
PSALM 9:9 HCSB

God is our protection and our strength.
He always helps in times of trouble.
PSALM 46:1 NCV

The LORD is a refuge for His people and a stronghold.
JOEL 3:16 NASB

I have learned in whatever state I am, to be content.
PHILIPPIANS 4:11 NKJV

A TIMELY TIP

No circumstances are too tough for God, and no problems are too big for Him. When times are tough, cast your burden upon Him, and He will give you the strength and courage you need to face any situation.

23

DIFFICULT RELATIONSHIPS

SOME RELATIONSHIPS ARE DANGEROUS TO YOUR EMOTIONAL HEALTH

*It is safer to meet a bear robbed of her cubs
than to confront a fool caught in foolishness.*
PROVERBS 17:12 NLT

Emotional health is contagious, and so is emotional distress. If you're fortunate enough to be surrounded by family members and friends who celebrate life and praise God, consider yourself profoundly blessed. But if you find yourself caught in an unhealthy relationship, it's time to look realistically at your situation.

In your dealings with difficult people, don't concern yourself too much with changing them; you can't do it. What you can do is to conduct yourself in a responsible fashion and insist that other people treat you with the dignity and consideration that you deserve.

In a perfect world filled with perfect people, our relationships, too, would be perfect, and our anxieties would be few and far between. But none of us are perfect and neither are our relationships . . . and that's okay. As we work to make our imperfect relationships a little happier and healthier, we grow as individuals and as families. But if we find ourselves in relationships that are debilitating or dangerous, then changes must be made, and soon.

If you find yourself caught up in a personal relationship that is bringing havoc into your life, and if you can't seem to find the courage to do something about it, don't hesitate to consult your pastor. Or you may choose to seek the advice of a trusted friend or a professionally trained counselor. But whatever you do, don't be satisfied with the status quo.

God has grand plans for your life; He has promised you the joy and abundance that can be yours through Him. But to fully experience God's gifts, you need happy, emotionally healthy people to share them with. It's up to you to make sure that you do your part to build the kinds of relationships that will bring abundance to you, to your family, and to God's world.

MORE THOUGHTS ABOUT DEALING WITH DISCOURAGING RELATIONSHIPS

Insults are like bad coins; we cannot help their being offered to us, but we need not take them.
C. H. SPURGEON

If you are having difficulty loving or relating to an individual, take him to God. Bother the Lord with this person. Don't you be bothered with him—leave him at the throne.
CHARLES SWINDOLL

We never get anywhere—nor do our conditions and circumstances change—when we look at the dark side of life.
LETTIE COWMAN

*Feelings of uselessness and hopelessness are not from God,
but from the evil one, the devil, who wants to discourage
you and thwart your effectiveness for the Lord.*

BILL BRIGHT

MORE FROM GOD'S WORD

*Give your burdens to the LORD, and he will take care of you.
He will not permit the godly to slip and fall.*

PSALM 55:22 NLT

God shall wipe away all the tears from their eyes.

REVELATION 7:17 KJV

The LORD is a refuge for His people and a stronghold.

JOEL 3:16 NASB

The LORD is near to those who have a broken heart.

PSALM 34:18 NKJV

If God is for us, who is against us?

ROMANS 8:31 HCSB

A TIMELY TIP

If you're having trouble dealing with a difficult person, don't be
discouraged and don't give up hope. There's always something you
can do to make your life better, even if it means breaking off the
relationship. Tough times never last, but determined, optimistic,
faith-filled people do.

24

DISAPPOINTMENTS

WHEN YOU'RE DISAPPOINTED, HE CAN HEAL YOUR HEART

Then they cried out to the LORD in their trouble,
and He saved them out of their distresses.
PSALM 107:13 NKJV

From time to time, all of us face life-altering, anxiety-increasing disappointments that leave us breathless. Oftentimes these disappointments come unexpectedly, leaving us with more questions than answers. But even when we don't have all the answers—or, for that matter, even when we don't seem to have *any* of the answers—God does. Whatever our circumstances, whether we stand atop the highest mountain or wander through the darkest valley, God is ready to protect us, to comfort us, and to heal us. Our task is to let Him.

When we are disheartened—on those cloudy days when our strength is sapped and our hope is shaken—there exists a source from which we can draw perspective and courage. That source is God. When we turn everything over to Him, we find that He is sufficient to meet our needs. No problem is too big for Him.

So the next time you feel discouraged or fearful, slow down long enough to have a serious talk with your Creator. Pray for guidance, pray for strength, and pray for the wisdom to trust your heavenly Father. Your troubles are temporary; His love is not.

MORE THOUGHTS ABOUT DEALING WITH DISAPPOINTMENTS

*Let God enlarge you when you are
going through distress. He can do it.*
WARREN WIERSBE

*If your hopes are being disappointed just now,
it means that they are being purified.*
OSWALD CHAMBERS

*In every difficult situation is potential value.
Believe this, then begin looking for it.*
NORMAN VINCENT PEALE

*We all have sorrows and disappointments, but one must
never forget that, if commended to God, they will issue in good.
His own solution is far better than any we could conceive.*
FANNY CROSBY

*Unless we learn to deal with disappointment,
it will rob us of joy and poison our souls.*
BILLY GRAHAM

Discouragement is the opposite of faith.
BILLY GRAHAM

More from God's Word

They that sow in tears shall reap in joy.
PSALM 126:5 KJV

He shall not be afraid of evil tidings:
his heart is fixed, trusting in the LORD.
PSALM 112:7 KJV

My son, do not despise the chastening
of the LORD, nor be discouraged
when you are rebuked by Him.
HEBREWS 12:5 NKJV

Many adversities come to
the one who is righteous, but the LORD
delivers him from them all.
PSALM 34:19 HCSB

He heals the brokenhearted and binds up their wounds.
PSALM 147:3 HCSB

A Timely Tip

When you're discouraged, disappointed, or hurt, don't spend too much time asking, "Why me, Lord?" Instead ask, "What now, Lord?" and then get busy. When you do, you'll feel better, stronger, and more confident.

25

DOUBT

WHEN YOU HAVE DOUBTS

Immediately the father of the child cried out and said with tears, "Lord, I believe; help my unbelief!"
MARK 9:24 NKJV

Doubts come in several shapes and sizes: doubts about God, doubts about the future, and doubts about your own abilities, for starters. And what, precisely, does God's Word say in response to these doubts? The Bible is clear: when we are beset by doubts, of whatever kind, we must draw ourselves nearer to God through worship and through prayer. When we do so, God, the loving Father who has never left our sides, draws ever closer to us (James 4:8).

Have you ever felt your faith in God slipping away? If so, you are not alone. Every life—including yours—is a series of successes and failures, celebrations and disappointments, joys and sorrows, hopes and doubts. Even the most faithful Christians are overcome by occasional bouts of fear and doubt. But even when you feel far removed from God, God never leaves your side, not for an instant. He is always with you, always willing to calm the storms of life. When you sincerely seek His presence—and when you genuinely seek to establish a deeper, more meaningful relationship with His

Son—God is prepared to touch your heart, to calm your fears, to answer your doubts, and to restore our soul.

MORE THOUGHTS ABOUT DEALING WITH DOUBTS

We are most vulnerable to the piercing winds of doubt when we distance ourselves from the mission and fellowship to which Christ has called us.
JONI EARECKSON TADA

Have you been tormented with fears and doubts? Bombarded with temptation to sin? Try praising the Lord, and watch Satan flee.
NANCY LEIGH DEMOSS

Ignoring Him by neglecting prayer and Bible reading will cause you to doubt.
ANNE GRAHAM LOTZ

Two types of voices command your attention today. Negative ones fill your mind with doubt, bitterness, and fear. Positive ones purvey hope and strength. Which one will you choose to heed?
MAX LUCADO

We never get anywhere—nor do our conditions and circumstances change—when we look at the dark side of life.
LETTIE COWMAN

More from God's Word

*Such doubters are thinking two different things
at the same time, and they cannot decide
about anything they do. They should not think
they will receive anything from the Lord.*
JAMES 1:7–8 NCV

In quietness and trust is your strength.
ISAIAH 30:15 NASB

*Those who trust in the LORD are like Mount Zion.
It cannot be shaken; it remains forever.*
PSALM 125:1 HCSB

*He must ask in faith without any doubting,
for the one who doubts is like the surf of the sea,
driven and tossed by the wind.*
JAMES 1:6 NASB

*Jesus said, "Don't let your hearts be troubled.
Trust in God, and trust in me."*
JOHN 14:1 NCV

A Timely Tip

Are doubts creeping in? If so, increase the amount of time you spend in Bible study, prayer, and worship. The more time you spend with God, the better you'll feel about your future and your faith.

26

EMOTIONAL SWINGS

LEARNING TO DEAL WITH
EMOTIONAL UPS AND DOWNS

*Should we accept only good things from
the hand of God and never anything bad?*
JOB 2:10 NLT

From time to time, all of us experience emotional swings. Even the most even-tempered among us experience natural human emotions such as anger, sadness, anxiety, and fear. Since we cannot eliminate these emotional highs and lows, we should seek to understand them. And we must learn to control our negative emotions before they control us.

When you encounter unfortunate circumstances that you cannot change, here's a proven way to retain your sanity: accept those circumstances (no matter how unpleasant), and trust God. American theologian Reinhold Niebuhr composed a profoundly simple verse that came to be known as the Serenity Prayer: "God, grant me the serenity to accept the things I cannot change, the courage to change the things I can, and the wisdom to know the difference." Niebuhr's words are far easier to recite than they are to live by. Why? Because most of us want life to unfold in accordance with our own wishes and timetables. But sometimes God has other plans. And if we learn to wait patiently for His plans to unfold, and if we learn to accept the things we simply cannot change, we'll deal more effectively with the ups and downs of life.

When we trust God completely and without reservation, we soon discover that our emotional swings are less dramatic and less painful. Then we can be comforted in the knowledge that our Creator is both loving and wise, and that He understands His plans perfectly, even when we do not.

MORE THOUGHTS ABOUT EMOTIONAL SWINGS

Treat pain and rage as visitors.
BEN HECHT

Bad temper is its own scourge. Few things are bitterer than to feel bitter. A man's venom poisons himself more than his victim.
CHARLES BUXTON

The truth is that even in the midst of trouble, happy moments swim by us every day, like shining fish waiting to be caught.
BARBARA JOHNSON

Find joy in the ordinary.
MAX LUCADO

Faith is the art of holding on to things your reason has once accepted in spite of your changing moods.
C. S. LEWIS

MORE FROM GOD'S WORD

Grow a wise heart—you'll do yourself a favor;
keep a clear head—you'll find a good life.
PROVERBS 19:8 MSG

For this very reason, make every effort to supplement
your faith with goodness, goodness with knowledge,
knowledge with self-control, self-control
with endurance, endurance with godliness.
2 PETER 1:5-6 HCSB

And let the peace of God rule in your hearts, to which
also you were called in one body; and be thankful.
COLOSSIANS 3:15 NKJV

All bitterness, anger and wrath, shouting and slander
must be removed from you, along with all malice.
And be kind and compassionate to one another,
forgiving one another, just as God also forgave you in Christ.
EPHESIANS 4:31-32 HCSB

A TIMELY TIP

If you're experiencing unrelenting anxiety or hurtful feelings that just won't go away, it's time to schedule an appointment with your pastor, a pastoral counselor, or a mental health professional. These people can help you look inside to discover, and then banish, the hurtful feelings or exaggerated thought patterns that may be triggering negative emotions and holding you back.

27

EMOTIONS ARE CONTAGIOUS

BEWARE: EMOTIONS ARE CONTAGIOUS

Bad temper is contagious—don't get infected.
PROVERBS 22:25 MSG

Emotional highs and lows are contagious. When we're surrounded by people with positive attitudes, we tend to think positively. But when we're surrounded by people whose emotions are negative, we get infected. Negative feelings can rob us of the peace and abundance that would otherwise be ours through Christ. When fear or anxiety separates us from the spiritual blessings that God has in store, we must rethink our priorities. And we must place faith above feelings.

Human emotions are highly variable, decidedly unpredictable, and often unreliable. Our emotions are like the weather, only sometimes far more fickle. As a consequence, we must learn to live by faith, not by the ups and downs of our neighbors' emotional roller coasters. So here's a question you should ask yourself: Who's pulling your emotional strings? Are you allowing highly emotional people or highly charged situations to dictate your moods, or are you wiser than that?

Sometime during the coming day, you may encounter a tough situation or a difficult person. And as a result, you may be gripped by a strong negative emotion. Distrust it. Rein it in. Test it. And turn it over to God. Your emotions will inevitably change; God will not. So trust Him completely. When you do, you'll be surprised at how quickly those negative feelings can evaporate into thin air.

MORE THOUGHTS ABOUT CONTAGIOUS EMOTIONS

Our emotions can lie to us, and we need to counter our emotions with truth.
BILLY GRAHAM

Our feelings do not affect God's facts.
AMY CARMICHAEL

A life lived in God is not lived on the plane of feelings, but of the will.
ELISABETH ELLIOT

If you desire to improve your physical well-being and your emotional outlook, increasing your faith can help you.
JOHN MAXWELL

It is Christ who is to be exalted, not our feelings. We will know Him by obedience, not by emotions. Our love will be shown by obedience, not by how good we feel about God at a given moment.
ELISABETH ELLIOT

More from God's Word

*Stay away from those who have foolish arguments
and talk about useless family histories and argue
and quarrel about the law. Those things
are worth nothing and will not help anyone.*
TITUS 3:9 NCV

*Fools give full vent to their rage,
but the wise bring calm in the end.*
PROVERBS 29:11 NIV

*Stop being angry! Turn from your rage!
Do not lose your temper—it only leads to harm.*
PSALM 37:8 NLT

*Mockers inflame a city,
but the wise turn away anger.*
PROVERBS 29:8 HCSB

Make no friendship with an angry man.
PROVERBS 22:24 NKJV

A Timely Tip

The friends you choose can make a profound impact on every aspect
of your life. So choose your friends carefully and prayerfully. And
remember that you have every right to select friends who contribute
to your spiritual and emotional health.

28

ENTHUSIASM

BE ENTHUSIASTIC!

*Whatever you do, do it enthusiastically,
as something done for the Lord and not for men.*
COLOSSIANS 3:23 HCSB

Can you truthfully say that you are an enthusiastic person? Are you passionate about your faith, your life, your family, and your future? Hopefully so. But if you ever find yourself caught in a web of anxiety and fear, it's time to recharge your spiritual batteries. And that means refocusing your priorities by putting God first.

Each day is a glorious opportunity to serve God and to do His will. Are you enthused about life, or do you struggle through each day giving scarcely a thought to God's blessings? Are you constantly praising God for His gifts, and are you sharing His Good News with the world? Are you excited about the possibilities for service that God has placed before you, whether at home, at work, or at church? You should be.

Norman Vincent Peale advised, "Get absolutely enthralled with something. Throw yourself into it with abandon. Get out of yourself. Be somebody. Do something." His words apply to you. So don't settle for a lukewarm existence and don't let your fears determine the direction of your life. Instead of sitting on the sidelines, become genuinely involved in life. The world needs your enthusiasm . . . and so do you.

More Thoughts about Enthusiasm

Those who have achieved excellence in the practice of an art or profession have commonly been motivated by great enthusiasm in their pursuit of it.
John Knox

Wherever you are, be all there. Live to the hilt every situation you believe to be the will of God.
Jim Elliot

Developing a positive attitude means working continually to find what is uplifting and encouraging.
Barbara Johnson

Two types of voices command your attention today. Negative ones fill your mind with doubt, bitterness, and fear. Positive ones purvey hope and strength. Which one will you choose to heed?
Max Lucado

Be enthusiastic. Every occasion is an opportunity to do good.
Russell Conwell

More from God's Word

Rejoice always! Pray constantly. Give thanks in everything, for this is God's will for you in Christ Jesus.
1 Thessalonians 5:16–18 HCSB

Let the hearts of those who seek the Lord rejoice. Look to the Lord and his strength; seek his face always.
1 Chronicles 16:10–11 NIV

A happy heart makes the face cheerful, but heartache crushes the spirit.
Proverbs 15:13 NIV

But as for me, I will hope continually, and will praise You yet more and more.
Psalm 71:14 NASB

Do your work with enthusiasm. Work as if you were serving the Lord, not as if you were serving only men and women.
Ephesians 6:7 NCV

A Timely Tip

Look upon your life as an exciting adventure because that's precisely what it can be *and* should be. Today and every day, your challenge is to maintain your enthusiasm for life, even when times are tough. So ask God to help you focus on His blessings, and don't let anybody or anything steal your joy.

29

ESTABLISHING BOUNDARIES

ESTABLISHING COMMON-SENSE BOUNDARIES

*Stay away from a fool, for you will
not find knowledge on their lips.*
PROVERBS 14:7 NIV

When you become involved in relationships that require you to compromise your values, you'll make yourself miserable. Why? Because when you find yourself in situations where other people are encouraging you to do things you know to be wrong, your guilty conscience simply won't allow you to be happy. And if you find yourself surrounded by people who are unstable, impulsive, or addicted, you'll soon discover that emotional distress is contagious, as are its consequences.

In a perfect world populated by perfect people, our relationships would be trouble free. But the world isn't perfect, and neither are the people who inhabit it. As a consequence, we occasionally find ourselves struggling in less-than-perfect relationships that make us anxious or fearful or both. As we work to make those imperfect relationships a little happier and healthier, we must first try to establish sensible boundaries. And if we find ourselves in relationships that are debilitating or dangerous, we should accept the fact that complete separation may be necessary.

To fully experience God's gifts, you need to establish sensible boundaries with people whose emotional challenges present threats to your emotional or physical health. After all, you deserve relationships that will bring abundance to you, to your family, and to God's world.

MORE THOUGHTS ABOUT BOUNDARIES

*You are justified in avoiding people who send you
from their presence with less hope and strength
to cope with life's problems than when you met them.*
ELLA WHEELER WILCOX

Stay away from fatty foods, hard liquor, and negative people.
MARIE T. FREEMAN

*Not everybody is healthy enough
to have a front-row seat in your life.*
SUSAN L. TAYLOR

It is far better to be alone than to be in bad company.
GEORGE WASHINGTON

No one can drive us crazy unless we give them the keys.
DOUG HORTON

More from God's Word

Walk with the wise and become wise;
associate with fools and get in trouble.
Proverbs 13:20 NLT

Be sober, be vigilant; because your
adversary the devil walks about like
a roaring lion, seeking whom he may devour.
1 Peter 5:8 NKJV

It is better to meet a bear robbed of her cubs
than to meet a fool doing foolish things.
Proverbs 17:12 NCV

Do not be deceived: "Bad company corrupts good morals."
1 Corinthians 15:33 HCSB

You are not the same as those who
do not believe. So do not join yourselves
to them. Good and bad do not belong together.
Light and darkness cannot share together.
2 Corinthians 6:14 NCV

A Timely Tip

You can't change other people, but you can change the way that you react to them. If someone is mistreating you, either physically or emotionally, you have the right to set boundaries and enforce those boundaries, even if it means separating yourself from that person.

30

FAITH

FAITH MAKES THE DIFFERENCE

He said unto her, Daughter, thy faith hath
made thee whole; go in peace, and be whole.
MARK 5:34 KJV

Because we live in a demanding world, all of us have mountains to climb and mountains to move. Moving those mountains requires faith. And the experience of trying to move mountains, with God's help, builds character.

Faith, like a tender seedling, can be nurtured or neglected. When we nurture our faith through prayer, meditation, and worship, God blesses our lives and lifts our spirits. But when we neglect to commune with the Father, we do ourselves and our loved ones a profound disservice.

When a suffering woman sought healing by merely touching the hem of His cloak, Jesus informed the woman that her faith in Him had healed her. The message to believers of every generation is clear: we must live by faith, not fear, and we must trust God in every aspect of our lives.

When you place your faith, your trust, indeed your life in the hands of Christ Jesus, you'll be amazed at the marvelous things He can do with you and through you. So strengthen your faith through praise, through worship, through Bible study, and through prayer. And trust God's plans. With Him, all things are possible, and He stands ready to open a world of possibilities to you *if* you have faith.

MORE THOUGHTS ABOUT MOUNTAIN-MOVING FAITH

Shout the shout of faith. Nothing can withstand the triumphant faith that links itself to omnipotence. The secret of all successful living lies in this shout of faith.
HANNAH WHITALL SMITH

I have learned that faith means trusting in advance what will only make sense in reverse.
PHILLIP YANCEY

Faith is not merely holding on to God. It is God holding on to you.
CORRIE TEN BOOM

Faith does not concern itself with the entire journey. One step is enough.
LETTIE COWMAN

Faith points us beyond our problems to the hope we have in Christ.
BILLY GRAHAM

More from God's Word

Don't be afraid. Only believe.
MARK 5:36 HCSB

All things are possible for the one who believes.
MARK 9:23 NCV

Don't be afraid, because I am your God.
I will make you strong and will help you;
I will support you with my right hand that saves you.
ISAIAH 41:10 NCV

Blessed are they that have not seen,
and yet have believed.
JOHN 20:29 KJV

For truly I say to you, if you have faith
the size of a mustard seed, you will say to this mountain,
"Move from here to there," and it will move;
and nothing will be impossible to you.
MATTHEW 17:20 NASB

A Timely Tip

Do you think you're in an impossible situation? If so, you're mistaken. You still have options, and God can still move mountains. Your job is to let Him.

31

FEAR

GOD IS BIGGER THAN YOUR DIFFICULTIES

Fear not, for I am with you; be not dismayed,
for I am your God. I will strengthen you, yes, I will help you,
I will uphold you with My righteous right hand.
ISAIAH 41:10 NKJV

All of us may find our courage tested by the inevitable disappointments and tragedies of life. After all, ours is a world filled with uncertainty, hardship, sickness, and danger. Old Man Trouble, it seems, is never too far from the front door.

When we focus upon our fears and our doubts, we may find many reasons to lie awake at night and fret about the uncertainties of the coming day. A better strategy, of course, is to focus not upon our fears but upon our God.

God is as near as your next breath, and He is in control. He offers salvation to all His children, including you. God is your shield and your strength; you are His forever. So don't focus your thoughts upon the fears of the day. Instead, trust God's plan and His eternal love for you. And remember: God is good, and He has the last word.

More Thoughts about Facing Your Fears

God shields us from most of the things we fear,
but when He chooses not to shield us,
He unfailingly allots grace in the measure needed.
ELISABETH ELLIOT

A perfect faith would lift us absolutely above fear.
GEORGE MACDONALD

The presence of fear does not mean
you have no faith. Fear visits everyone.
But make your fear a visitor and not a resident.
MAX LUCADO

It is good to remind ourselves
that the will of God comes from the
heart of God and that we need not be afraid.
WARREN WIERSBE

God's power is great enough for
our deepest desperation. You can go on.
You can pick up the pieces and start anew.
You can face your fears. You can find peace
in the rubble. There is healing for your soul.
SUZANNE DALE EZELL

MORE FROM GOD'S WORD

But He said to them, "It is I; do not be afraid."
JOHN 6:20 NKJV

*Even though I walk through the darkest valley,
I will fear no evil, for you are with me;
your rod and your staff, they comfort me.*
PSALM 23:4 NIV

*The LORD is my light and my salvation—
whom should I fear? The LORD is the stronghold of my life—
of whom should I be afraid?*
PSALM 27:1 HCSB

*Peace I leave with you; My peace I give to you;
not as the world gives do I give to you.
Do not let your heart be troubled, nor let it be fearful.*
JOHN 14:27 NASB

Be not afraid, only believe.
MARK 5:36 KJV

A TIMELY TIP

Are you feeling anxious or fearful? If so, trust God to handle those problems that are simply too big for you to solve. Entrust the future—your future—to God. The two of you, working together, can accomplish great things for His kingdom.

32

FEAR OF CHANGE

DEALING WITH CHANGE

*To every thing there is a season, and a time
to every purpose under the heaven.*
ECCLESIASTES 3:1 KJV

In our fast-paced world, everyday life has become an exercise in managing change. Our circumstances change; our relationships change; our bodies change. We grow older every day, as does our world. So it's no wonder that so many of us feel anxious and afraid. Thankfully, God does not change. He is eternal, as are the truths that are found in His holy Word.

Is the world spinning a little too fast for your liking? Are you facing difficult circumstances or unwelcome changes? If so, please remember that God is far bigger than any problem you may face. So, instead of worrying about life's inevitable challenges, put your faith in the Father and His only begotten Son. After all, "Jesus Christ is the same yesterday, today, and forever" (Hebrews 13:8 NKJV). And it is precisely because your Savior does not change that you can face your challenges with courage for today and hope for tomorrow.

Are you anxious about situations that you cannot control? Take your anxieties to God. Are you fearful? Take your fears to Him.

Does your little corner of the universe seem to be trembling beneath your feet? Seek protection from the One who cannot be moved. The same God who created the universe will protect you if you ask Him . . . so ask Him . . . and then serve Him with willing hands and a trusting heart.

MORE THOUGHTS ABOUT DEALING WITH CHANGE

Conditions are always changing; therefore, I must not be dependent upon conditions. What matters supremely is my soul and my relationship to God.
CORRIE TEN BOOM

Christians are supposed not merely to endure change, nor even to profit by it, but to cause it.
HARRY EMERSON FOSDICK

We must change in order to survive.
PEARL BAILEY

Change is the only constant in maturity.
EDWIN LOUIS COLE

Successful and happy living is built into you by God who created you. If you have never experienced this kind of life, maybe you need to be recreated.
NORMAN VINCENT PEALE

You can endure change by pondering His permanence.
MAX LUCADO

More from God's Word

The wise see danger ahead and avoid it,
but fools keep going and get into trouble.
PROVERBS 22:3 NCV

Then He who sat on the throne said,
"Behold, I make all things new."
REVELATION 21:5 NKJV

But grow in the grace and knowledge
of our Lord and Savior Jesus Christ.
To Him be the glory both now and forever. Amen.
2 PETER 3:18 NKJV

When I was a child, I spoke like a child,
I thought like a child, I reasoned like a child.
When I became a man, I put aside childish things.
1 CORINTHIANS 13:11 HCSB

I am the LORD, and I do not change.
MALACHI 3:6 NLT

A Timely Tip

Change is inevitable. Growth is not. God will come to your doorstep on countless occasions with opportunities to learn and to grow, and He will knock. Your challenge, of course, is to open the door.

33

FEAR OF FAILURE

DON'T LET THE FEAR OF FAILURE
HOLD YOU BACK

For though the righteous fall seven times, they rise again.
PROVERBS 24:16 NIV

As we consider the uncertainties of the future, we are confronted with a powerful temptation: the temptation to play it safe. Unwilling to move mountains, we fret over molehills. Unwilling to entertain great hopes for tomorrow, we focus on the unfairness of today. Unwilling to trust God completely, we take timid half-steps when God intends that we make giant leaps. Why are we willing to settle for baby steps when God wants us to leap tall buildings in a single bound? Because we are fearful that we might fail.

The occasional disappointments and failures of life are inevitable. Such setbacks are simply the price that we must occasionally pay for our willingness to take risks as we follow our dreams. But even when we encounter bitter disappointments, we must never lose faith. And we must remember that in the game of life, we never hit a home run unless we are willing to step up to the plate and swing.

Hebrews 10:36 advises, "Patient endurance is what you need now, so that you will continue to do God's will. Then you will receive all that he has promised" (NLT). These words remind us that when we persevere, we will eventually receive the rewards that God has promised us. What's required is perseverance, not perfection.

When we face disappointments or unfortunate circumstances, God stands ready to protect us. Our responsibility, of course, is to ask Him for protection. And while we are waiting for God's plans to unfold, we can be comforted in the knowledge that our Creator can overcome any obstacle, even if we cannot.

Today, ask God for the courage to step beyond the boundaries of your self-doubts. Ask Him to guide you to a place where you can realize your full potential—a place where you are freed from the fear of failure. Ask Him to do His part, and promise Him that you will do your part. Don't ask Him to lead you to a "safe" place; ask Him to lead you to the "right" place . . . and remember: those two places are seldom the same.

MORE THOUGHTS ABOUT THE FEAR OF FAILURE

No matter how badly we have failed, we can always get up and begin again. Our God is the God of new beginnings.
WARREN WIERSBE

No amount of falls will really undo us if we keep picking ourselves up after each one.
C. S. LEWIS

Those who have failed miserably are often the first to see God's formula for success.
ERWIN LUTZER

Failure is one of life's most powerful teachers.
How we handle our failures determines whether
we're going to simply "get by" in life or "press on."
BETH MOORE

MORE FROM GOD'S WORD

The LORD is near to those who have a broken heart.
PSALM 34:18 NKJV

If you listen to correction to improve your life,
you will live among the wise.
PROVERBS 15:31 NCV

We are hard-pressed on every side, yet not crushed;
we are perplexed, but not in despair.
2 CORINTHIANS 4:8 NKJV

Weeping may endure for a night,
but joy comes in the morning.
PSALM 30:5 NKJV

A TIMELY TIP

Setbacks are inevitable, but your response to them is optional, so don't give up and don't lose hope. You and the Lord, working together, can always find a way to turn a stumbling block into a stepping stone, which means that better days will arrive, and perhaps sooner than you think.

34

FEAR OF MISTAKES

DON'T BE TOO HARD ON YOURSELF

He who covers his sins will not prosper, but whoever confesses and forsakes them will have mercy.
PROVERBS 28:13 NKJV

Everybody makes mistakes, and so will you. In fact, Winston Churchill once observed, "Success is going from failure to failure without loss of enthusiasm." What was good for Churchill is also good for you. You should expect to make mistakes—plenty of mistakes—but you should not allow those missteps to rob you of the enthusiasm you need to fulfill God's plan for your life.

We are imperfect people living in an imperfect world; occasional blunders are simply part of the price we pay for being here. But even though mistakes are an inevitable part of life's journey, repeated mistakes should not be. When we commit those inevitable missteps, we must correct them, learn from them, and pray for the wisdom not to repeat them. When we do, our mistakes become lessons, and our lives become adventures in growth, not stagnation.

Have you made a mistake or two or three? Of course you have. But here's the big question: Have you used your mistakes as stumbling blocks or stepping stones? The answer to that question will determine the quality of your day and the quality of your life.

More Thoughts about Mistakes

*By the mercy of God, we may repent
a wrong choice and alter the consequences
by making a right choice.*

A. W. Tozer

*Every misfortune, every failure,
every loss may be transformed.
God has the power to transform
all misfortunes into "God-sends."*

Lettie Cowman

*God is able to take mistakes,
when they are committed to Him,
and make of them something
for our good and for His glory.*

Ruth Bell Graham

*Mistakes offer the possibility for
redemption and a new start in God's kingdom.
No matter what you're guilty of,
God can restore your innocence.*

Barbara Johnson

*It is human to err, but it is devilish
to remain willfully in error.*

St. Augustine

More from God's Word

If we confess our sins to him, he is faithful and just to forgive us our sins and to cleanse us from all wickedness.
1 John 1:9 NLT

Therefore, if anyone is in Christ, he is a new creation; old things have passed away; behold, all things have become new.
2 Corinthians 5:17 NKJV

Therefore let us approach the throne of grace with boldness, so that we may receive mercy and find grace to help us at the proper time.
Hebrews 4:16 HCSB

Be merciful, just as your Father is merciful.
Luke 6:36 NIV

The mercy of the LORD is from everlasting to everlasting upon them that fear him, and his righteousness unto children's children.
Psalm 103:17 KJV

A Timely Tip

Everybody makes mistakes, and so will you. When you fall short of your expectations, don't overreact and don't be too hard on yourself. Instead, try to learn something, try to make amends, and try to move on as quickly as possible.

35

FEAR OF REJECTION

YOU CAN'T PLEASE EVERYBODY
(NOR SHOULD YOU TRY)

For am I now trying to win the favor of people, or God?
Or am I striving to please people? If I were still
trying to please people, I would not be a slave of Christ.
GALATIANS 1:10 HCSB

If you're like most people, you'd like to gain the admiration of your neighbors, your coworkers, and, most importantly, your family members. Some people, however, are impossible to please, and other people want you to please them by doing things that are contrary to your faith. It's perfectly natural to want to please other people, but you should never allow the fear of their rejection to overshadow your eagerness to please God.

Would you like a time-tested formula for successful relationships? Here is a formula that is proven and true: in every relationship you establish, seek God's approval first. Does this sound too simple? Perhaps it is simple, but it is also the only way to reap the marvelous riches that the Lord has in store for you.

The nineteenth-century reformer Margaret Fuller warned, "Beware of over-great pleasure in being popular or even beloved."

And her words still ring true. Few things in life are more futile than trying to please other people for the wrong reasons. When we place God in a position of secondary importance, we do ourselves great harm. But when we imitate Jesus and place the Lord in His rightful place—at the center of our lives—then we claim spiritual treasures that will endure forever.

Who will you try to please today: God or man? Your primary obligation is not to please imperfect men and women. Your obligation is to strive diligently to meet the expectations of an all-knowing and perfect God. Trust Him always. Love Him always. Praise Him always. And seek to please Him. Always.

MORE THOUGHTS ABOUT THE FEAR OF REJECTION

*Popularity is far more dangerous
for the Christian than persecution.*
BILLY GRAHAM

*The major problem with letting others define you
is that it borders on idolatry. Your concern to please
others dampens your desire to please your Creator.*
SARAH YOUNG

*Don't pay much attention to who is for you
and who is against you. This is your major concern:
that God be with you in everything you do.*
THOMAS À KEMPIS

It's about time we stopped buying things we don't need with money we don't have to impress people we don't like.

ADRIAN ROGERS

MORE FROM GOD'S WORD

The fear of man is a snare, but the one who trusts in the LORD is protected.
PROVERBS 29:25 HCSB

Keep your eyes focused on what is right, and look straight ahead to what is good.
PROVERBS 4:25 NCV

My son, if sinners entice you, don't be persuaded.
PROVERBS 1:10 HCSB

Do not be unequally yoked together with unbelievers. For what fellowship has righteousness with lawlessness? And what communion has light with darkness?
2 CORINTHIANS 6:14 NKJV

A TIMELY TIP

If you are burdened with a people-pleasing personality, it's now officially time to outgrow it. In other words, it's time to realize that you can't please all of the people all of the time, nor should you attempt to.

36

FEAR OF THE FUTURE

For I know the thoughts that I think toward you,
says the LORD, thoughts of peace and not of evil,
to give you a future and a hope. Then you will call
upon Me and go and pray to Me, and I will listen to you.
JEREMIAH 29:11–12 NKJV

Sometimes, when the future seems daunting, we are gripped by unfounded fears and unwarranted anxieties. We lose sight, at least temporarily, of the fact that God's promises never fail and that we, His children, are protected.

It is inevitable that we will face disappointments and failures while we are here on earth, but these are only temporary defeats. This world can be a place of trials and tribulations, but when we place our trust in the Giver of all things good, we are secure. God has promised us peace, joy, and eternal life. And God keeps His promises today, tomorrow, and forever.

Are you willing to place your future in the hands of a loving and all-knowing God? Do you trust in the ultimate goodness of His plan for your life? Will you face today's challenges with optimism and hope? You should. After all, God created you for a very important purpose: His purpose. And you still have important work to do: His work.

Today, as you live in the present and look to the future, remember that God has a plan for you. Act—and believe—accordingly.

More Thoughts about Your Very Bright Future

Never be afraid to trust an unknown future to a known God.
Corrie ten Boom

Knowing that your future is absolutely assured can free you to live abundantly today.
Sarah Young

Our future may look fearfully intimidating, yet we can look up to the Engineer of the Universe, confident that nothing escapes His attention or slips out of the control of those strong hands.
Elisabeth Elliot

Seeking God first will always put us in the correct position and aim us in the right direction to move into the future God has for us.
Stormie Omartian

Trust the past to God's mercy, the present to God's love, and the future to God's providence.
St. Augustine

Our prospects are as bright as the promises of God.
Adoniram Judson

More from God's Word

There is surely a future hope for you,
and your hope will not be cut off.
PROVERBS 23:18 NIV

The LORD is my light and my salvation—
whom should I fear? The LORD is the stronghold of my life—
of whom should I be afraid?
PSALM 27:1 HCSB

But if we look forward to something we don't have yet,
we must wait patiently and confidently.
ROMANS 8:25 NLT

Wisdom is pleasing to you. If you find it,
you have hope for the future.
PROVERBS 24:14 NCV

Rest in God alone, my soul, for my hope comes from Him.
PSALM 62:5 HCSB

A Timely Tip

Hope for the future is simply one aspect of trusting God. When you seek God's guidance in every aspect of your life, your future is secure. So don't worry too much about the distant future. Instead, remember that whatever tomorrow holds, God will be there, and you'll be protected.

37

FOLLOWING CHRIST

FOLLOW IN HIS FOOTSTEPS
AS CLOSELY AS YOU CAN

Then He said to them all, "If anyone wants to come with Me,
he must deny himself, take up his cross daily, and follow Me."
LUKE 9:23 HCSB

Whom will you walk with today? Are you going to walk with people who worship the ways of the world? Or are you going to walk with the Son of God? Jesus walks with you. Are you walking with Him? Hopefully you will choose to walk with Him today and every day of your life.

Jesus loved you so much that He endured unspeakable humiliation and suffering for you. How will you respond to Christ's sacrifice? Will you take up your cross and follow Him (Luke 9:23) or will you choose another path? When you place your hopes squarely at the foot of the cross, when you place Jesus squarely at the center of your life, you will be blessed.

The nineteenth-century writer Hannah Whitall Smith observed, "The crucial question for each of us is this: What do you think of Jesus, and do you yet have a personal acquaintance with Him?" Indeed, the answer to that question determines the quality, the course, and the direction of our lives today and for all eternity.

Today provides another glorious opportunity to place yourself in the service of the One from Galilee. May you seek His will, may you trust His Word, and may you walk in His footsteps—now and forever—amen.

MORE THOUGHTS ABOUT FOLLOWING CHRIST

A disciple is a follower of Christ. That means you take on His priorities as your own. His agenda becomes your agenda. His mission becomes your mission.
CHARLES STANLEY

Be assured, if you walk with Him and look to Him, and expect help from Him, He will never fail you.
GEORGE MUELLER

Jesus gives us hope because He keeps us company, has a vision, and knows the way we should go.
MAX LUCADO

Choose Jesus Christ! Deny yourself, take up the cross, and follow Him, for the world must be shown. The world must see, in us, a discernible, visible, startling difference.
ELISABETH ELLIOT

Christ is not valued at all unless He is valued above all.
ST. AUGUSTINE

MORE FROM GOD'S WORD

*Whoever is not willing to carry the cross and follow me
is not worthy of me. Those who try to hold on to their
lives will give up true life. Those who give up
their lives for me will hold on to true life.*
MATTHEW 10:38–39 NCV

*Walk in a manner worthy of the God
who calls you into His own kingdom and glory.*
1 THESSALONIANS 2:12 NASB

*Take my yoke upon you, and learn of me; for I am meek
and lowly in heart: and ye shall find rest unto your souls.
For my yoke is easy, and my burden is light.*
MATTHEW 11:29-30 KJV

For we walk by faith, not by sight.
2 CORINTHIANS 5:7 HCSB

*But whoever keeps His word, truly in him the love of God is
perfected. This is how we know we are in Him: The one who
says he remains in Him should walk just as He walked.*
1 JOHN 2:5–6 HCSB

A TIMELY TIP

When you follow in Christ's footsteps—when you honor Him with
your thoughts, your actions, and your prayers—you can be sure that
you're always on the right path.

38

FOLLOWING YOUR CONSCIENCE

LISTEN CAREFULLY TO YOUR CONSCIENCE CLEAR

*So I strive always to keep my conscience
clear before God and man.*
ACTS 24:16 NIV

Few things in life torment us more than a guilty conscience. And few things in life provide more contentment than the knowledge that we are obeying God's commandments. A clear conscience is one of the rewards we earn when we obey God's Word and follow His will. When we follow God's will and accept His gift of salvation, our earthly rewards are never ceasing, and our heavenly rewards are everlasting.

Billy Graham correctly observed, "Most of us follow our conscience as we follow a wheelbarrow. We push it in front of us in the direction we want to go." If that describes you, then here's a word of warning: both you and your wheelbarrow may be heading for trouble, and fast.

You can sometimes keep secrets from other people, but you can never keep secrets from God. God knows what you think and what you do. And if you want to please Him, you must start with good intentions, a pure heart, and a clear conscience.

If you sincerely desire to live a life that is pleasing to God, you must follow His commandments. When you do, you'll quickly discover that your anxieties and fears will begin to subside. And your clear conscience will be an additional blessing because you'll never need to look over your shoulder to see who—besides God—is watching.

MORE THOUGHTS ABOUT TRUSTING YOUR CONSCIENCE

God speaks through a variety of means. In the present God primarily speaks by the Holy Spirit, through the Bible, prayer, circumstances, and the church.
HENRY BLACKABY

Conscience is God's voice to the inner man.
BILLY GRAHAM

The conscience is a built-in warning system that signals us when something we have done is wrong.
JOHN MACARTHUR

It is neither safe nor prudent to do anything against conscience.
MARTIN LUTHER

Conscience can only be satisfied if God is satisfied.
C. H. SPURGEON

More from God's Word

Behold, the kingdom of God is within you.
LUKE 17:21 KJV

*Let us come near to God with a sincere heart
and a sure faith, because we have been
made free from a guilty conscience,
and our bodies have been washed with pure water.*
HEBREWS 10:22 NCV

*Create in me a clean heart, O God;
and renew a right spirit within me.*
PSALM 51:10 KJV

*People's thoughts can be like
a deep well, but someone with
understanding can find the wisdom there.*
PROVERBS 20:5 NCV

*Now the goal of our instruction is love that comes
from a pure heart, a good conscience, and a sincere faith.*
1 TIMOTHY 1:5 HCSB

A Timely Tip

When your conscience speaks, listen carefully. If you consistently live in accordance with your beliefs, God will guide your steps, and you'll be secure.

39

FORGIVENESS

BE QUICK TO FORGIVE

*Above all, love each other deeply,
because love covers a multitude of sins.*
1 PETER 4:8 NIV

The world holds few if any rewards for those who remain angrily focused upon the past. Still, the act of forgiveness is difficult for all but the most saintly men and women. Are you mired in the emotional quicksand of bitterness or regret? If so, you are not only disobeying God's Word, you are also wasting your time.

Being frail, fallible, imperfect human beings, most of us are quick to anger, quick to blame, slow to forgive, and even slower to forget. Yet as Christians, we are commanded to forgive others, just as we, too, have been forgiven.

If there exists even one person—alive or dead—against whom you hold bitter feelings, it's time to forgive. Or if you are embittered against yourself for some past mistake or shortcoming, it's finally time to forgive yourself and move on. Hatred, bitterness, and regret are not part of God's plan for your life. Forgiveness is.

MORE THOUGHTS
ABOUT FORGIVENESS

*Forgiveness is one of the most beautiful words
in the human vocabulary. How much pain could
be avoided if we all learned the meaning of this word!*

BILLY GRAHAM

*Forgiveness is an act of the will,
and the will can function regardless
of the temperature of the heart.*

CORRIE TEN BOOM

*Forgiveness does not change the past,
but it does enlarge the future.*

DAVID JEREMIAH

Look upon the errors of others in sorrow, not in anger.

HENRY WADSWORTH LONGFELLOW

*In one bold stroke, forgiveness
obliterates the past and permits us
to enter the land of new beginnings.*

BILLY GRAHAM

Forgiveness is God's command.

MARTIN LUTHER

More from God's Word

Blessed are the merciful, because they shall receive mercy.
MATTHEW 5:7 HCSB

But I say to you, love your enemies,
and pray for those who persecute you.
MATTHEW 5:44 NASB

And whenever you stand praying, if you have anything
against anyone, forgive him, so that your Father
in heaven may also forgive you your wrongdoing.
MARK 11:25 HCSB

And be kind to one another, tenderhearted, forgiving one
another, even as God in Christ forgave you.
EPHESIANS 4:32 NKJV

Judge not, and you shall not be judged. Condemn not, and you
shall not be condemned. Forgive, and you will be forgiven.
LUKE 6:37 NKJV

A Timely Tip

Forgiveness is its own reward. Bitterness is its own punishment. Bitter thoughts are bad for your spiritual and emotional health. Guard your words and thoughts accordingly.

40

GOD'S ABUNDANCE

GOD WANTS YOU
TO LIVE ABUNDANTLY

*I have come that they may have life,
and that they may have it more abundantly.*
JOHN 10:10 NKJV

God has a plan for every facet of your life, and His plan includes provisions for your spiritual, physical, and emotional health. But He expects you to do your fair share of the work. In a world that is populated by imperfect people, you may find it all too easy to respond impulsively, thus making matters even worse. A far better strategy, of course, is to ask for God's guidance. And you can be sure that whenever you ask for God's help, He will give it.

God's Word promises that He will support you in good times and comfort you in hard times. The Creator of the universe stands ready to give you the strength to meet any challenge and the courage to deal effectively with difficult circumstances. When you ask for God's help, He responds in His own way and at His own appointed hour. But make no mistake: He always responds.

Today, as you encounter the challenges of everyday life, remember that your heavenly Father never leaves you, not even for a moment.

He's always available, always ready to listen, always ready to lead. When you make a habit of talking to Him early and often, He'll guide you and comfort you every day of your life.

MORE THOUGHTS ABOUT ABUNDANCE

Jesus wants Life for us; Life with a capital L.
JOHN ELDREDGE

God loves you and wants you to experience peace and life—abundant and eternal.
BILLY GRAHAM

God is the giver, and we are the receivers. And His richest gifts are bestowed not upon those who do the greatest things, but upon those who accept His abundance and His grace.
HANNAH WHITALL SMITH

Every difficult task that comes across your path— every one that you would rather not do, that will take the most effort, cause the most pain, and be the greatest struggle—brings a blessing with it.
LETTIE COWMAN

Knowing that your future is absolutely assured can free you to live abundantly today.
SARAH YOUNG

More from God's Word

May Yahweh bless you and protect you; may Yahweh make His face shine on you, and be gracious to you.
Numbers 6:24–25 HCSB

And God is able to make all grace abound to you, so that always having all sufficiency in everything, you may have an abundance for every good deed.
2 Corinthians 9:8 NASB

My cup runs over. Surely goodness and mercy shall follow me all the days of my life; and I will dwell in the house of the LORD forever.
Psalm 23:5–6 NKJV

Success, success to you, and success to those who help you, for your God will help you.
1 Chronicles 12:18 NIV

Until now you have asked for nothing in My name. Ask and you will receive, that your joy may be complete.
John 16:24 HCSB

A Timely Tip

God's blessings are always available. Even when you're dealing with a situation that has caused you to feel anxious or afraid, the Lord is constantly offering you His abundance and His peace. So remember that you can still find peace amid the storm if you guard your thoughts, do your best, and leave the rest up to Him.

41

GOD'S GUIDANCE

LET GOD BE YOUR GUIDE

*Trust in the LORD with all your heart, and lean not
on your own understanding; in all your ways
acknowledge Him, and He shall direct your paths.*

PROVERBS 3:5–6 NKJV

If you're dealing with anxiety, irrational fears, or other negative emotions, you need God's guidance. And of this you can be sure: if you seek His guidance, He will give it.

C. S. Lewis observed, "I don't doubt that the Holy Spirit guides your decisions from within when you make them with the intention of pleasing God. The error would be to think that He speaks only within, whereas in reality He speaks also through Scripture, the Church, Christian friends, and books." These words remind us that God has many ways to make Himself known. Our challenge is to make ourselves open to His instruction.

If you're wise, you'll form the habit of speaking to God early and often. But you won't stop there—you'll also study God's Word, you'll obey God's commandments, and you'll associate with people who do likewise.

So if you're unsure of your next step, lean upon God's promises and lift your prayers to Him. Remember that God is always near—always trying to get His message through. Open yourself to Him every day, and trust Him to guide your path. When you do, you'll be protected today, tomorrow, and forever.

MORE THOUGHTS ABOUT GOD'S GUIDANCE

When we are obedient,
God guides our steps and our stops.
CORRIE TEN BOOM

God never leads us to do anything
that is contrary to the Bible.
BILLY GRAHAM

Get into the habit of dealing with God about everything.
OSWALD CHAMBERS

Are you serious about wanting God's guidance
to become a personal reality in your life?
The first step is to tell God that you know you can't
manage your own life; that you need His help.
CATHERINE MARSHALL

The will of God will never take us
where the grace of God cannot sustain us.
BILLY GRAHAM

MORE FROM GOD'S WORD

The LORD says, "I will guide you along the best pathway
for your life. I will advise you and watch over you."
PSALM 32:8 NLT

Shew me thy ways, O LORD; teach me thy paths.
Lead me in thy truth, and teach me: for thou art
the God of my salvation; on thee do I wait all the day.
PSALM 25:4–5 KJV

Teach me to do Your will, for You are my God;
Your Spirit is good. Lead me in the land of uprightness.
PSALM 143:10 NKJV

Morning by morning he wakens me
and opens my understanding to his will.
The Sovereign LORD has spoken to me, and I have listened.
ISAIAH 50:4–5 NLT

Yet LORD, You are our Father; we are the clay,
and You are our potter; we all are the work of Your hands.
ISAIAH 64:8 HCSB

A TIMELY TIP

Need direction? Let God be your guide. When your emotions are frayed—or if you feel like you're losing control—call time out and pray for guidance. When you seek it, God will give it.

42

GOD'S PLAN

HE HAS A PLAN FOR YOU

As it is written: What eye did not see and ear did not hear,
and what never entered the human mind—
God prepared this for those who love Him.

1 CORINTHIANS 2:9 HCSB

Do you want to experience a life filled with abundance, peace, and emotional stability? If so, here's a word of warning: you'll need to resist the temptation to do things "your way" and commit, instead, to do things God's way.

God has plans for your life. Big plans. But He won't force you to follow His will; to the contrary, He has given you free will, the ability to make decisions on your own. With the freedom to choose comes the responsibility of living with the consequences of the choices you make.

When you make the decision to seek God's will for your life, you will contemplate His Word, and you will be watchful for His signs. You will associate with fellow believers who will encourage your spiritual growth. And you will listen to that inner voice that speaks to you in the quiet moments of your daily devotionals.

Sometimes God's plans are crystal clear, but other times He

leads you through the wilderness before He delivers you to the Promised Land. So be patient, keep searching, and keep praying. If you do, then in time God will answer your prayers and make His plans known. The Lord intends to use you in wonderful, unexpected ways. You'll discover those plans by doing things His way . . . and you'll be eternally grateful that you did.

MORE THOUGHTS ABOUT GOD'S PLAN

Every experience God gives us, every person
He brings into our lives, is the perfect preparation
for the future that only He can see.
CORRIE TEN BOOM

God has a course mapped out for your life,
and all the inadequacies in the world will not change
His mind. He will be with you every step of the way.
CHARLES STANLEY

God's purpose is greater than our problems,
our pain, and even our sins.
RICK WARREN

If not a sparrow falls upon the ground
without your Father, you have reason to see
the smallest events of your career are arranged by Him.
C. H. SPURGEON

MORE FROM GOD'S WORD

*We must do the works of Him who sent Me while it is day.
Night is coming when no one can work.*
JOHN 9:4 HCSB

*And yet, O LORD, you are our Father. We are the clay,
and you are the potter. We are all formed by your hand.*
ISAIAH 64:8 NLT

*It is God who is at work in you,
both to will and to work for His good pleasure.*
PHILIPPIANS 2:13 NASB

*For whoever does the will of God
is My brother and My sister and mother.*
MARK 3:35 NKJV

*For My thoughts are not your thoughts, and your ways
are not My ways. . . . For as heaven is higher
than earth, so My ways are higher than your ways,
and My thoughts than your thoughts.*
ISAIAH 55:8–9 HCSB

A TIMELY TIP

Even when you're feeling anxious or afraid, you can be sure that God
has a wonderful plan for your life. And the time to start looking for
that plan—and living it—is now. Discovering God's plan begins
with prayer, but it doesn't end there. You've also got to work at it.

43

GOD'S PRESENCE

GOD IS ALWAYS WITH YOU

Draw near to God, and He will draw near to you.
JAMES 4:8 HCSB

If God is everywhere, why does He sometimes seem so far away? The answer to that question, of course, has nothing to do with God and everything to do with us. When we begin each day on our knees, in praise and worship to Him, God often seems very near indeed. But if we ignore God's presence or, worse yet, rebel against it altogether, the world in which we live can become a spiritual and emotional wasteland.

Are you tired, discouraged, or fearful? Be comforted because God is with you. Are you anxious or confused? Listen to the quiet voice of your heavenly Father. Are you bitter? Talk with God and seek His guidance. Are you celebrating a great victory? Thank God and praise Him. He is the Giver of all things good.

In whatever condition you find yourself, wherever you are, whether you are happy or sad, victorious or vanquished, troubled or triumphant, celebrate God's presence. And be comforted. God is not just near. He is here.

MORE THOUGHTS ABOUT GOD'S PRESENCE

*It is God to whom and with whom
we travel, and while He is the end
of our journey, He is also at every stopping place.*
ELISABETH ELLIOT

*Do not limit the limitless God!
With Him, face the future unafraid
because you are never alone.*
LETTIE COWMAN

*God is an infinite circle
whose center is everywhere.*
ST. AUGUSTINE

*Mark it down. You will
never go where God is not.*
MAX LUCADO

*The Lord is the one who travels
every mile of the wilderness way
as our leader, cheering us, supporting
and supplying and fortifying us.*
ELISABETH ELLIOT

MORE FROM GOD'S WORD

I am not alone, because the Father is with Me.
JOHN 16:32 NKJV

Be still, and know that I am God.
PSALM 46:10 KJV

*Though I walk through the valley
of the shadow of death, I will fear no evil:
for thou art with me.*
PSALM 23:4 KJV

*I know the LORD is always with me.
I will not be shaken, for he is right beside me.*
PSALM 16:8 NLT

*The eyes of Yahweh roam throughout
the earth to show Himself strong
for those whose hearts are completely His.*
2 CHRONICLES 16:9 HCSB

A TIMELY TIP

The next time you feel a flood of negative emotions coming on, take a deep breath and remind yourself that God isn't far away. He's right here, right now. And He's willing to talk to you right here, right now.

44

GOD'S PROMISES

TRUST GOD'S PROMISES

As for God, his way is perfect: the word of the LORD is tried:
he is a buckler to all those that trust in him.

PSALM 18:30 KJV

In the eighteenth psalm, David teaches us that God is trustworthy. Simply put, when God makes a promise, He keeps it.

So what do you expect from the day ahead? Are you willing to trust God completely or are you living beneath a cloud of doubt and fear? God's Word makes it clear: you should trust Him and His promises, and when you do, you can live courageously.

For thoughtful Christians, every day begins and ends with God's Son and God's promises. When we accept Christ into our hearts, God promises us the opportunity for earthly peace and spiritual abundance. But more importantly, God promises us the priceless gift of eternal life.

Sometimes, especially when we find ourselves caught in the inevitable entanglements of life, we fail to trust God completely.

Are you tired? Discouraged? Fearful? Be comforted and trust the promises that God has made to you. Are you worried or anxious? Be confident in God's power. Do you see a difficult future ahead?

Be courageous and call upon God. He will protect you and then use you according to His purposes. Are you confused? Listen to the quiet voice of your heavenly Father. He is not a God of confusion. Talk with Him; listen to Him; trust Him, and trust His promises. He is steadfast, and He is your Protector, now and forever.

More Thoughts about God's Promises

Let God's promises shine on your problems.
CORRIE TEN BOOM

The Bible is God's book of promises, and unlike the books of man, it does not change or go out of date.
BILLY GRAHAM

Beloved, God's promises can never fail to be accomplished, and those who patiently wait can never be disappointed, for a believing faith leads to realization.
LETTIE COWMAN

Gather the riches of God's promises. Nobody can take away from you those texts from the Bible which you have learned by heart.
CORRIE TEN BOOM

Don't let obstacles along the road to eternity shake your confidence in God's promises.
DAVID JEREMIAH

More from God's Word

He heeded their prayer,
because they put their trust in him.
1 CHRONICLES 5:20 NKJV

Sustain me as You promised, and I will live;
do not let me be ashamed of my hope.
PSALM 119:116 HCSB

My God is my rock, in whom I take refuge,
my shield and the horn of my salvation.
2 SAMUEL 22:3 NIV

They will bind themselves
to the LORD with an eternal covenant
that will never be broken.
JEREMIAH 50:5 NLT

Let us hold on to the confession
of our hope without wavering,
for He who promised is faithful.
HEBREWS 10:23 HCSB

A Timely Tip

God has made many promises to you, and He will keep every single
one of them. Your job is to trust God's Word and to live accordingly.

45

GOD'S PROTECTION

HE IS OUR SHEPHERD

The LORD is my shepherd, I shall not want.
He makes me lie down in green pastures;
He leads me beside quiet waters. He restores my soul.
PSALM 23:1–3 NASB

God knows everything about His creation. Whether we're enjoying happy days or challenging ones, the Creator watches over us and protects us.

The Lord is our greatest refuge. When every earthly support system fails, He remains steadfast, and His love remains unchanged. When we encounter life's inevitable disappointments and setbacks, the Father remains faithful. When we experience anxiety or fear, He is always with us, always ready to respond to our prayers, always working in us and through us to turn trouble into triumph.

Thankfully, even when there's nowhere else to turn, we can turn our thoughts and prayers to the Lord, and He will respond. Even during life's most difficult days, God stands by us. Our job, of course, is to return the favor and stand by Him.

MORE THOUGHTS ABOUT GOD'S PROTECTION

Measure the size of the obstacles against the size of God.
BETH MOORE

*Only believe, don't fear. Our Master,
Jesus, always watches over us, and no matter what
the persecution, Jesus will surely overcome it.*
LOTTIE MOON

*A mighty fortress is our God,
a bulwark never failing, our helper
He amid the flood of mortal ills prevailing.*
MARTIN LUTHER

*The safest place in all the world
is in the will of God, and the safest protection
in all the world is the name of God.*
WARREN WIERSBE

*Discipline yourself to stay close to God.
He alone is your security.*
BILLY GRAHAM

*Faith is not merely holding on to God.
It is God holding on to you.*
CORRIE TEN BOOM

MORE FROM GOD'S WORD

The LORD is my light and my salvation—
whom should I fear? The LORD is the stronghold
of my life—of whom should I be afraid?
PSALM 27:1 HCSB

Those who trust in the LORD are like Mount Zion.
It cannot be shaken; it remains forever.
PSALM 125:1 HCSB

As for God, His way is perfect; the word of the LORD is proven;
He is a shield to all who trust in Him.
PSALM 18:30 NKJV

The LORD is my rock, my fortress, and my deliverer,
my God, my mountain where I seek refuge. My shield, the horn
of my salvation, my stronghold, my refuge, and my Savior.
2 SAMUEL 22:2–3 HCSB

So we may boldly say: "The Lord is my helper;
I will not fear. What can man do to me?"
HEBREWS 13:6 NKJV

A TIMELY TIP

God has promised to protect you, and He's going to keep that promise. So if you're worried or afraid, pray for guidance and pray for a trusting heart. You need both, and He will give you both *if* you ask.

46

GOD'S TIMING

TRUST GOD'S TIMING

Therefore humble yourselves under the mighty hand of God,
that He may exalt you in due time.
1 PETER 5:6 NKJV

If you're experiencing tough times, you're undoubtedly eager for things to improve. Perhaps you've prayed about your situation but seen no results. If so, keep praying, keep working, and be patient.

The Bible teaches us to trust God's timing in all matters, but we are sorely tempted to do otherwise, especially when our hearts are breaking. We pray (and trust) that we will find peace someday, and we want it now. God, however, works on His own timetable, and His schedule does not always coincide with ours.

God's plans are perfect; ours most certainly are not. Thus we must learn to trust the Father in good times and hard times. So today, as you meet the challenges of everyday life, do your best to turn everything over to God. Whatever your problem, He can solve it. And you can be sure that He will solve it when the time is right.

More Thoughts about God's Timing

*Waiting on God brings us to the journey's end
quicker than our feet.*

LETTIE COWMAN

*Teach us, O Lord, the disciplines of patience,
for to wait is often harder than to work.*

PETER MARSHALL

*We must learn to move according
to the timetable of the Timeless One,
and to be at peace.*

ELISABETH ELLIOT

*The Christian's journey through
life isn't a sprint but a marathon.*

BILLY GRAHAM

*We often hear about waiting on God,
which actually means that He is waiting
until we are ready. There is another side,
however. When we wait for God,
we are waiting until He is ready.*

LETTIE COWMAN

More from God's Word

To every thing there is a season,
and a time to every purpose under the heaven.
ECCLESIASTES 3:1 KJV

He has made everything appropriate in its time.
He has also put eternity in their hearts, but man cannot
discover the work God has done from beginning to end.
ECCLESIASTES 3:11 HCSB

Trust in the LORD with all your heart, and lean not
on your own understanding; in all your ways
acknowledge Him, and He shall direct your paths.
PROVERBS 3:5–6 NKJV

The LORD longs to be gracious to you; therefore he will
rise up to show you compassion. For the LORD
is a God of justice. Blessed are all who wait for him!
ISAIAH 30:18 NIV

Those who trust in the LORD are like Mount Zion.
It cannot be shaken; it remains forever.
PSALM 125:1 HCSB

A Timely Tip

If you're waiting patiently for the Lord to help you resolve a difficult situation, remember this: God is never early or late; He's always on time. Although you don't know precisely what you need or when you need it, He does. So trust His timing.

47

GRIEF

WHEN YOU GRIEVE, HE OFFERS COMFORT

Weeping may endure for a night,
but joy comes in the morning.
PSALM 30:5 NKJV

Grief visits all of us who live long and love deeply. When we lose a loved one, or when we experience profound loss, darkness overwhelms us for a while, and it seems as if our purpose for living has vanished. Thankfully, God has other plans.

The Christian faith, as communicated through the words of the Holy Bible, is a healing faith. It offers comfort in times of trouble, courage for our fears, hope instead of hopelessness. For Christians, the grave is not a final resting place, it is a place of transition. Through the healing words of God's promises, Christians understand that the Lord continues to manifest His plan in good times and bad.

God intends that you have a meaningful, abundant life, but He expects you to do your part in claiming those blessings. So as you work through your grief, you will find it helpful to utilize all the resources that God has placed along your path. God makes help available, but it's up to you to find it and then to accept it.

First and foremost, you should lean upon the love, help, and support of family members, friends, fellow church members, and your pastor. Other resources include the following:

- various local counseling services, including, but not limited to, pastoral counselors, psychologists, and community mental health facilities
- group counseling programs that deal with your specific loss
- your personal physician
- the local bookstore or library (which will contain specific reading material about your grief and about your particular loss)

If you are experiencing the intense pain of a recent loss, or if you are still mourning a loss from long ago, perhaps you are now ready to begin the next stage of your journey with God. If so, be mindful of this fact: as a wounded survivor, you will have countless opportunities to serve others. And by serving others, you will bring purpose and meaning to the suffering you've endured.

MORE THOUGHTS ABOUT SADNESS AND GRIEF

God is sufficient for all our needs, for every problem, for every difficulty, for every broken heart, for every human sorrow.
PETER MARSHALL

Despair is always the gateway of faith.
OSWALD CHAMBERS

God has enough grace to solve every dilemma you face, wipe every tear you cry, and answer every question you ask.
MAX LUCADO

MORE FROM GOD'S WORD

The Lord shall give thee rest from thy sorrow, and from thy fear.
ISAIAH 14:3 KJV

The LORD is near to those who have a broken heart.
PSALM 34:18 NKJV

Ye shall be sorrowful, but your sorrow shall be turned into joy.
JOHN 16:20 KJV

He heals the brokenhearted and binds up their wounds.
PSALM 147:3 HCSB

Blessed are the poor in spirit: for theirs is the kingdom of heaven. Blessed are they that mourn: for they shall be comforted.
MATTHEW 5:3–4 KJV

A TIMELY TIP

Grief is not meant to be avoided or feared; it is meant to be worked through. Grief hurts, but denying your true feelings can hurt even more. With God's help—and with time—you can face your pain and move beyond it.

48

GUARDING YOUR HEART

GOD WANTS YOU TO
GUARD YOUR HEART

Guard your heart above all else, for it is the source of life.
PROVERBS 4:23 HCSB

You live in a world filled with high-anxiety messages that can provoke fear and discouragement. Whether you're standing in line at the checkout counter or checking social media, you're bombarded by a near-endless stream of distractions and subtle temptations that seem to be woven into the fabric of everyday life. Yet God's Word is clear: we are to guard our hearts "above all else." So how should we respond to the difficult people and troubling circumstances that complicate our lives and rouse our emotions? We must react fairly, honestly, maturely, and we must never betray our Christian beliefs.

Life is a series of conscious decisions and unconscious choices. Each day, we make countless decisions that can bring us closer to God . . . or not. When we guard our hearts—and when we live in accordance with God's commandments—we earn His blessings. So as followers of Christ, we must remain vigilant. Not only must we resist Satan when he confronts us, but we must also avoid the people and the places where Satan can most easily tempt us.

Do you seek God's peace and His blessings? Then guard your heart. When you're tempted to lash out in anger, hold your tongue. When you're faced with a difficult choice or a powerful temptation, seek God's counsel and trust the counsel He gives. When you're anxious or afraid, take a deep breath, calm yourself, and follow in the footsteps of God's only begotten Son. Invite God into your heart and live according to His commandments. When you do, you will be blessed today, and tomorrow, and forever.

MORE THOUGHTS ABOUT GUARDING YOUR HEART FROM EVIL

There is no neutral ground in the universe:
every square inch, every split second,
is claimed by God and counterclaimed by Satan.
C. S. LEWIS

Our fight is not against any physical enemy; it is against
organizations and powers that are spiritual. We must struggle
against sin all our lives, but we are assured we will win.
CORRIE TEN BOOM

Our battles are first won or lost in the secret places of
our will in God's presence, never in full view of the world.
OSWALD CHAMBERS

No matter how many pleasures Satan offers you, his ultimate
intention is to ruin you. Your destruction is his highest priority.
ERWIN LUTZER

More from God's Word

*Finally, brothers and sisters, whatever is true, whatever is noble,
whatever is right, whatever is pure, whatever is lovely,
whatever is admirable—if anything is excellent
or praiseworthy—think about such things.*
PHILIPPIANS 4:8 NIV

*Flee from youthful passions, and pursue righteousness,
faith, love, and peace, along with those
who call on the Lord from a pure heart.*
2 TIMOTHY 2:22 HCSB

*The one who keeps God's commands lives in him,
and he in them. And this is how we know that he lives in us:
We know it by the Spirit he gave us.*
1 JOHN 3:24 NIV

*The peace of God, which surpasses all understanding,
will guard your hearts and minds through Christ Jesus.*
PHILIPPIANS 4:7 NKJV

A Timely Tip

God wants you to guard your heart from situations or harmful
emotions that would drive you away from Him. He wants the best
for you, and you, of course, want the same for yourself. How do you
achieve the best life has to offer? You should start by guarding your
heart against the inevitable temptations and countless distractions
that threaten your spiritual and emotional health.

49

GUILT

DON'T LET GUILT RULE YOUR LIFE

*Blessed are those who don't feel guilty
for doing something they have decided is right.*
ROMANS 14:22 NLT

All of us have sinned. Sometimes our sins result from our own stubborn rebellion against God's commandments. And sometimes we are swept up in events that are beyond our ability to control. Under either set of circumstances, we may experience intense feelings of guilt. But God has an answer for the guilt that we feel. That answer, of course, is His forgiveness. When we confess our wrong-doings and repent from them, we are forgiven by the One who created us.

Are you troubled by feelings of guilt or regret? Are you focused so intently on yesterday that your vision of today is clouded? If so, you still have work to do—spiritual work. You must atone for your mistakes the best you can, and you must ask your heavenly Father for His forgiveness. When you do so, He will forgive you completely and without reservation. Then, you must forgive yourself just as the Lord has forgiven you: thoroughly and unconditionally.

God's forgiveness is permanent. And if He, in His infinite wisdom, has forgiven your sins, how then can you withhold forgiveness from yourself? The answer, of course, is that once God has forgiven you, you should forgive yourself too. When you forgive yourself once and for all, you'll stop investing energy in those most useless of emotions: bitterness, regret, and self-recrimination. Then you can get busy making the world a better place, and that's as it should be. After all, since God has forgiven you, isn't it about time that you demonstrate your gratitude by serving Him?

MORE THOUGHTS ABOUT GUILT

The purpose of guilt is to bring us to Jesus. Once we are there, then its purpose is finished. If we continue to make ourselves guilty—to blame ourselves—then that is a sin in itself.
CORRIE TEN BOOM

Forgiveness is an opportunity that God extended to us on the cross. When we accept His forgiveness and are willing to forgive ourselves, then we find relief.
BILLY GRAHAM

Guilt is an appalling waste of energy; you can't build on it. It's only good for wallowing in.
KATHERINE MANSFIELD

The redemption, accomplished for us by our Lord Jesus Christ on the cross at Calvary, is redemption from the power of sin as well as from its guilt. Christ is able to save all who come unto God by Him.
HANNAH WHITALL SMITH

More from God's Word

Let us come near to God with a sincere heart and a sure faith,
because we have been made free from a guilty conscience,
and our bodies have been washed with pure water.
HEBREWS 10:22 NCV

Create in me a pure heart, God,
and make my spirit right again.
PSALM 51:10 NCV

How can I know all the sins lurking in my heart?
Cleanse me from these hidden faults. Keep your servant
from deliberate sins! Don't let them control me.
Then I will be free of guilt and innocent of great sin.
PSALM 19:12–13 NLT

Be gracious to me, God, according to Your faithful love;
according to Your abundant compassion, blot out my rebellion.
Wash away my guilt, and cleanse me from my sin.
PSALM 51:1–2 HCSB

A Timely Tip

Guilt is an emotion that can be debilitating. If you're being plagued by guilt, remember this: if you've asked for God's forgiveness, He has already given it. So if the Creator has forgiven you, why are you unwilling to forgive yourself? When you answer that question honestly, you'll realize that God's forgiveness gives you permission to forgive yourself and move on.

50

HAPPINESS

YES, YOU CAN BE HAPPY

Those who listen to instruction will prosper;
those who trust the LORD will be joyful.
PROVERBS 16:20 NLT

Do you seek happiness, abundance, and contentment? And do you seek these things now, not later? If so, here's what you should do: love God and His Son; depend upon God for strength; try, to the best of your ability, to follow His will; and strive to obey His holy Word. When you do these things, you'll discover that happiness goes hand in hand with obedience.

The happiest people are not those who resist God's instruction or intentionally rebel against Him; the happiest people are those who love God and obey His commandments. So if you sincerely want to be happy, you should behave accordingly.

What should you expect from the upcoming day? A world full of possibilities (of course it's up to you to seize them), and God's promise of abundance (of course it's up to you to accept it). So as you prepare for the next step in your life's journey, remember this: obedience to God doesn't ensure instant happiness, but disobedience to God always makes genuine happiness impossible.

More Thoughts about Happiness

*The practical effect of Christianity is happiness,
therefore let it be spread abroad everywhere!*
C. H. Spurgeon

*The truth is that even in the midst
of trouble, happy moments swim by us every day,
like shining fish waiting to be caught.*
Barbara Johnson

*Happiness is a thing that comes and goes.
It can never be an end in itself.
Holiness, not happiness, is the end of man.*
Oswald Chambers

*Happy is the person who has
learned the secret of being content
with whatever life brings him.*
Billy Graham

*The world looks for happiness
through self-assertion. The Christian knows
that joy is found in self-abandonment.*
Elisabeth Elliot

Joy comes not from what we have but what we are.
C. H. Spurgeon

More from God's Word

Happiness makes a person smile,
but sadness can break a person's spirit.
PROVERBS 15:13 NCV

Joyful is the person who finds wisdom,
the one who gains understanding.
PROVERBS 3:13 NLT

I have come that they may have life,
and that they may have it more abundantly.
JOHN 10:10 NKJV

A joyful heart is good medicine,
but a broken spirit dries up the bones.
PROVERBS 17:22 HCSB

If they obey and serve him, they will
spend the rest of their days in prosperity
and their years in contentment.
JOB 36:11 NIV

A Timely Tip

The best day to be happy is this one. Even if you're dealing with troublesome emotions, even if you're caught up in difficult situation, you have many reasons to celebrate, so don't delay. Let the celebration begin today. Make up your mind to be happy, and ask God to help you make the choice to rejoice.

51

HOPE

NEVER LOSE HOPE

*Let us hold fast the confession of our hope without wavering,
for He who promised is faithful.*

HEBREWS 10:23 NASB

On the darkest days of our lives, we may be confronted with an illusion that seems very real indeed: the illusion of hopelessness. Try though we might, we simply can't envision a solution to our problems—and we fall into the darkness of despair. During these times, we may question God—His love, His presence, even His very existence. Despite God's promises, despite Christ's love, and despite our many blessings, we may envision little or no hope for the future. These dark days can be dangerous times for us and for our loved ones.

If you find yourself falling into the spiritual traps of anxiety, fear, and discouragement, seek the encouraging words of fellow Christians and the healing touch of Jesus. After all, it was Christ who promised, "These things I have spoken unto you, that in me ye might have peace. In the world ye shall have tribulation: but be of good cheer; I have overcome the world" (John 16:33 KJV).

Can you place your future into the hands of a loving and all-knowing God? Can you live amid the uncertainties of today, knowing that God has dominion over all your tomorrows? Can you summon the faith to trust God in good times and hard times? If you can, you are wise and you are blessed.

Once you've made the decision to trust God completely, it's time to get busy. The willingness to take action—even if the outcome of that action is uncertain—is an effective way to combat hopelessness. When you decide to roll up your sleeves and begin solving your own problems, you'll feel empowered, and you may see the first real glimmer of hope.

So today and every day, ask God for these things: clear perspective, mountain-moving faith, and the courage to do what needs doing. After all, no problem is too big for God. Through Him, all things are possible.

MORE THOUGHTS ABOUT HOPE

The earth's troubles fade in the light of heaven's hope.
BILLY GRAHAM

*The presence of hope in the invincible
sovereignty of God drives out fear.*
JOHN PIPER

*Of course you will encounter trouble. But behold a God of
power who can take any evil and turn it into a door of hope.*
CATHERINE MARSHALL

*Jesus gives us hope because He keeps us company,
has a vision, and knows the way we should go.*
MAX LUCADO

More from God's Word

*Be strong and courageous, all you who
put your hope in the LORD.*
PSALM 31:24 HCSB

*I say to myself, "The LORD is mine,
so I hope in him."*
LAMENTATIONS 3:24 NCV

Hope deferred makes the heart sick.
PROVERBS 13:12 NKJV

*The LORD is good to those who wait for Him,
to the soul who seeks Him. It is good
that one should hope and wait quietly
for the salvation of the LORD.*
LAMENTATIONS 3:25–26 NKJV

*This hope we have as an anchor of the soul,
a hope both sure and steadfast.*
HEBREWS 6:19 NASB

A Timely Tip

If you're worried about dealing with a difficult situation, don't give up hope, and don't stop looking for a better solution to your problem. Instead of procrastinating, tackle the problem now. You and God, working together, can do amazing things. So be hopeful and get busy.

52

JOY

BE JOYFUL!

Rejoice in the Lord always. Again I will say, rejoice!
PHILIPPIANS 4:4 NKJV

The joy that the world offers is fleeting and incomplete: here today, gone tomorrow, not coming back anytime soon. But God's joy is different. His joy has staying power. In fact, it's a gift that never stops giving to those who welcome His Son into their hearts.

Psalm 100 reminds us to celebrate the life that God has given us: "Shout for joy to the LORD, all the earth. Worship the LORD with gladness; come before Him with joyful songs" (vv. 1–2 NIV). Yet sometimes, amid the inevitable complications and predicaments that are woven into the fabric of everyday life, we forget to rejoice. Instead of celebrating life, we complain about it. This is an understandable mistake, but a mistake nonetheless. As Christians, we are called by our Creator to live joyfully and abundantly. To do otherwise is to squander His spiritual gifts.

This day and every day, Christ offers you His peace and His joy. Accept it and share it with others, just as He has shared His joy with you.

More Thoughts about Joy

Joy is the great note all throughout the Bible.
OSWALD CHAMBERS

*Joy is the direct result of having God's
perspective on our daily lives and the effect
of loving our Lord enough to obey
His commands and trust His promises.*
BILL BRIGHT

*Joy is the settled assurance that God is
in control of all the details of my life,
the quiet confidence that ultimately everything
is going to be all right, and the determined
choice to praise God in all things.*
KAY WARREN

Joy comes not from what we have but what we are.
C. H. SPURGEON

*The greatest honor you can give
Almighty God is to live gladly and joyfully
because of the knowledge of His love.*
JULIAN OF NORWICH

*When we get rid of inner conflicts
and wrong attitudes toward life,
we will almost automatically burst into joy.*
E. STANLEY JONES

More from God's Word

So you also have sorrow now.
But I will see you again. Your hearts will rejoice,
and no one will rob you of your joy.
JOHN 16:22 HCSB

Until now you have asked for nothing
in My name. Ask and you will receive,
that your joy may be complete.
JOHN 16:24 HCSB

I have spoken these things to you
so that My joy may be in you
and your joy may be complete.
JOHN 15:11 HCSB

This is the day which the LORD
has made; let us rejoice and be glad in it.
PSALM 118:24 NASB

A Timely Tip

Joy does not depend upon your circumstances; it depends upon your thoughts and upon your relationship with God. Every day, the Lord gives you many reasons to rejoice. The gifts are His, but the rejoicing is up to you.

53

LISTENING TO GOD

LISTENING CAREFULLY TO GOD

Come to me with your ears wide open.
Listen, and you will find life.
ISAIAH 55:3 NLT

Sometimes God displays His wishes in ways that are undeniable. But on other occasions, the Lord's messages are much more subtle. Sometimes God speaks to us in quiet tones, and when He does, we are well advised to listen carefully.

Do you take time each day for an extended period of silence? And during those precious moments, do you sincerely open your heart to your Creator? If so, you are wise and you are blessed.

The world can be a noisy place, a place filled to the brim with distractions, interruptions, and frustrations. And if you're not careful, the struggles and stresses of everyday living can rattle your emotions and rob you of the peace that should rightfully be yours because of your personal relationship with Christ. So take time each day to quietly commune with your Savior. When you do, you will most certainly encounter the subtle hand of God, and if you are wise, you will let Him lead you along the path that He has chosen.

More Thoughts about Listening to God

Prayer begins by talking to God,
but it ends in listening to Him.
In the face of Absolute Truth,
silence is the soul's language.
Fulton J. Sheen

If you, too, will learn to wait upon God,
to get alone with Him, and remain silent
so that you can hear His voice when
He is ready to speak to you, what a difference
it will make in your life!
Kay Arthur

Deep within the center of the soul
is a chamber of peace where God lives and where,
if we will enter it and quiet all the other sounds,
we can hear His gentle whisper.
Lettie Cowman

God's voice is still and quiet and easily
buried under an avalanche of clamor.
Charles Stanley

When God speaks to us,
He should have our full attention.
Billy Graham

More from God's Word

Be silent before Me.
ISAIAH 41:1 HCSB

*In quietness and in confidence
shall be your strength.*
ISAIAH 30:15 KJV

*The one who is from God listens
to God's words. This is why you don't listen,
because you are not from God.*
JOHN 8:47 HCSB

Rest in the LORD, and wait patiently for Him.
PSALM 37:7 NKJV

Be still, and know that I am God.
PSALM 46:10 KJV

A Timely Tip

In every stage of life, and in every circumstance, God has important things He's trying to teach you. So listen carefully to your conscience; pay attention to the things you learn in the Bible; and try to learn something new every day. When you do, God will guide you and protect you.

54

LONELINESS

WHEN YOU'RE LONELY

I am not alone, because the Father is with me.
JOHN 16:32 KJV

If you're like most people, you've experienced occasional bouts of loneliness. If so, you understand the genuine pain that accompanies those feelings that "nobody cares." In truth, lots of people care about you, but at times you may hardly notice their presence.

Sometimes intense feelings of loneliness can be the result of clinical depression. In such cases, it's time to seek professional help. Other times, however, your feelings of loneliness may come as a result of your own hesitation: the hesitation to get out there and make new friends.

The world is teeming with people who are looking for new friends. And yet, ironically enough, too many of us allow our friendships to wither away, not because we intentionally alienate others but because we simply don't pay enough attention to them.

Ralph Waldo Emerson advised, "The only way to have a friend is to be one." Emerson realized that a lasting relationship, like a beautiful garden, must be tended with care. Here are a few helpful tips on tending the garden of friendship . . . and reaping a bountiful harvest:

- Remember the first rule of friendship: it's the golden one, and it starts like this: "Do unto others . . ." (Matthew 7:12).
- If you're trying to make new friends, become interested in them . . . and eventually they'll become interested in you (Colossians 3:12).
- Take the time to reconnect with old friends: they'll be glad you did, and so, too, will you (Philippians 1:3).
- Become more involved in your church or in community service: they'll welcome your participation, and you'll welcome the chance to connect with more and more people (1 Peter 5:2).

MORE THOUGHTS ABOUT FRIENDSHIP

Friendship is one of the sweetest joys of life.
Many might have failed beneath the bitterness
of their trial had they not found a friend.
C. H. SPURGEON

A friend is one who makes me do my best.
OSWALD CHAMBERS

What is a friend? A single soul dwelling in two bodies.
ST. AUGUSTINE

I cannot even imagine where I would be
today were it not for that handful of friends
who have given me a heart full of joy.
Let's face it: friends make life a lot more fun.
CHARLES SWINDOLL

It is not darkness you are going to,
for God is Light. It is not lonely, for Christ is with you.
It is not unknown country, for Christ is there.

CHARLES KINGSLEY

MORE FROM GOD'S WORD

A friend loves at all times,
and a brother is born for a time of adversity.
PROVERBS 17:17 NIV

As iron sharpens iron, so people can improve each other.
PROVERBS 27:17 NCV

Oil and incense bring joy to the heart,
and the sweetness of a friend is better than self-counsel.
PROVERBS 27:9 HCSB

It is good and pleasant when God's people live together in peace!
PSALM 133:1 NCV

Dear friends, if God loved us in this way,
we also must love one another.
1 JOHN 4:11 HCSB

A TIMELY TIP

If you're feeling lonely, it's a signal that you need to reach out. Remember that God is close by, and so is someone who needs your help. If you find someone to help, you won't be lonely for long.

55

MAINTAINING PERSPECTIVE

KEEPING THINGS IN PERSPECTIVE

*Since you have been raised to new life with Christ,
set your sights on the realities of heaven, where Christ
sits in the place of honor at God's right hand.*

COLOSSIANS 3:1 NLT

For most of us, life is busy and complicated. Amid the rush and crush of the daily grind, it is easy to lose perspective . . . it's easy, but it's wrong. When our emotions seem to have been hijacked and the world seems to be spinning out of control, we can regain perspective by slowing ourselves down and then turning our thoughts and prayers toward God.

Do you carve out quiet moments each day to offer thanksgiving and praise to your Creator? You should. During these moments of stillness, you will often sense the love and wisdom of our Lord. When you call upon the Lord and prayerfully seek His will, He will give you wisdom and perspective. When you make God's priorities your priorities, He will direct your steps and calm your fears.

So today and every day hereafter, pray for a sense of balance and perspective. And remember: no challenges are too big for God—and that includes yours.

More Thoughts about Maintaining Perspective

God's peace and perspective are available to you through His Word.
ELIZABETH GEORGE

Look at everything as though you are seeing it for the first or last time, then your time on earth will be filled with glory.
BETTY SMITH

Perspective is everything when you are experiencing the challenges of life.
JONI EARECKSON TADA

Joy is the direct result of having God's perspective on our daily lives and the effect of loving our Lord enough to obey His commands and trust His promises.
BILL BRIGHT

The world appears very little to a soul that contemplates the greatness of God.
BROTHER LAWRENCE

More from God's Word

Trust in the LORD with all your heart
and lean not on your own understanding.
PROVERBS 3:5 NIV

If you teach the wise, they will get knowledge.
PROVERBS 21:11 NCV

Teach me, LORD, the meaning of Your statutes,
and I will always keep them.
PSALM 119:33 HCSB

The one who acquires good sense loves himself;
one who safeguards understanding finds success.
PROVERBS 19:8 HCSB

Joyful is the person who finds wisdom,
the one who gains understanding.
PROVERBS 3:13 NLT

A Timely Tip

When you focus on the world, you lose perspective. When you focus on God's promises and His love, you gain clearer perspective. To keep things in perspective, focus on God and on His plans for your life.

56

MAKING PEACE WITH THE PAST

MAKE PEACE WITH YOUR PAST

*One thing I do, forgetting those things which
are behind and reaching forward to those things
which are ahead, I press toward the goal
for the prize of the upward call of God in Christ Jesus.*

PHILIPPIANS 3:13–14 NKJV

Because you are human, you may be slow to forget yesterday's disappointments. But if you sincerely seek to focus your hopes and energies on the future, then you must find ways to accept the past, no matter how difficult it may be to do so.

Have you made peace with your past? If so, congratulations. But if you are mired in the quicksand of bitterness or regret, it's time to plan your escape. How can you do so? By accepting what has been and by trusting God for what will be. You must also forgive those who have hurt you and learn the lessons that hard times have taught you.

So if you have not yet made peace with the past, today is the day to declare an end to all hostilities. When you do, you can then turn your thoughts to the wondrous promises of God and to the glorious future that He has in store for you.

More Thoughts about Making Peace with Your Past

*Trust the past to God's mercy, the present
to God's love and the future to God's providence.*
St. Augustine

*Our yesterdays present irreparable things to us;
it is true that we have lost opportunities which
will never return, but God can transform this destructive
anxiety into a constructive thoughtfulness for the future.*
Oswald Chambers

*Don't waste energy regretting the way
things are or thinking about what
might have been. Start at the present moment—
accepting things exactly as they are—
and search for My way in the midst
of those circumstances.*
Sarah Young

*Don't be bound by the past and its failures.
But don't forget its lessons either.*
Billy Graham

*Who you are in Christ is far more important and meaningful
than whatever has taken place in your past.*
Elizabeth George

More from God's Word

*Do not remember the former things, nor consider
the things of old. Behold, I will do a new thing.*
ISAIAH 43:18–19 NKJV

*He restoreth my soul: he leadeth me
in the paths of righteousness for his name's sake.*
PSALM 23:3 KJV

*Have mercy on me, O God, according to
your unfailing love; according to your
great compassion blot out my transgressions.
Wash away all my iniquity and cleanse me from my sin.*
PSALM 51:1–2 NIV

*Your old sinful self has died,
and your new life is kept with Christ in God.*
COLOSSIANS 3:3 NCV

*And He who sits on the throne said,
"Behold, I am making all things new."*
REVELATION 21:5 NASB

A Timely Tip

The past is past. Don't invest all your mental energy there. If you're focusing on yesterday, it's time to change your focus. If you're living in the past, move on while there's still time. If you're carrying a grudge against someone, it's time to forgive.

57

MANAGING ANXIETY

MANAGING ANXIETY

Cast all your anxiety on him because he cares for you.
1 PETER 5:7 NIV

Ours is an anxious generation. We live in an uncertain world, a world where tragedies can befall the most righteous (and the most innocent) among us. Yet even on those difficult days when our anxieties threaten to overwhelm us, we can be assured that God stands ready to protect us. Psalm 147 promises, "He heals the broken-hearted and bandages their wounds" (v. 3 NCV). So when we are troubled or anxious, we must call upon the Lord, and in His own time and according to His own plan, He will heal us.

Sometimes our anxieties may stem from physical causes—chemical reactions in the brain that produce severe emotional distress or crippling panic attacks. In such cases, modern medicine offers hope to those who suffer. But oftentimes our anxieties result from spiritual deficits, not physical ones. And when we're spiritually depleted, the best prescription is found not in the medicine cabinet but deep inside the human heart. What we need is a higher daily dose of God's love, God's peace, God's assurance, and God's presence. And how do we acquire these blessings from our Creator? Through prayer, through meditation, through worship, and through trust.

Prayer is a powerful antidote to anxiety; so too is a regular time of devotional reading and meditation. When we spend quiet moments in the divine presence of our heavenly Father, we are reminded once again that our troubles are temporary but His love is not.

As you face the inevitable challenges of everyday living, do you find yourself becoming anxious, troubled, discouraged, or fearful? If so, turn every one of your concerns over to your heavenly Father. The same God who created the universe will comfort you if you ask Him. Your job, simply put, is to ask Him.

MORE THOUGHTS ABOUT ANXIETY

*Worry and anxiety are sand in
the machinery of life; faith is the oil.*
E. STANLEY JONES

*So often we pray and then fret anxiously,
waiting for God to hurry up and do something.
All the while God is waiting for us to calm down,
so He can do something through us.*
CORRIE TEN BOOM

*Some people feel guilty about their anxieties
and regard them as a defect of faith, but they are afflictions,
not sins. Like all afflictions, they are,
if we can so take them, our share in the passion of Christ.*
C. S. LEWIS

Every tomorrow has two handles: We can take hold
of the handle of anxiety or the handle of faith.
HENRY WARD BEECHER

MORE FROM GOD'S WORD

Therefore do not worry about tomorrow,
for tomorrow will worry about its own things.
Sufficient for the day is its own trouble.
MATTHEW 6:34 NKJV

Peace I leave with you; My peace I give to you;
not as the world gives do I give to you.
Do not let your heart be troubled, nor let it be fearful.
JOHN 14:27 NASB

Let not your heart be troubled;
you believe in God, believe also in Me.
JOHN 14:1 NKJV

Cast your burden on the LORD, and He shall sustain you;
He shall never permit the righteous to be moved.
PSALM 55:22 NKJV

A TIMELY TIP

If anxious feelings become debilitating—or if you're unable to sleep because of racing thoughts or irrational worries—consult your physician. Your anxiety may have physical causes that are contributing to your distress. Help is available. Ask for it.

58

MANAGING EMOTIONS

LEARNING TO KEEP
EMOTIONS IN CHECK

Grow a wise heart—you'll do yourself a favor;
keep a clear head—you'll find a good life.
PROVERBS 19:8 MSG

Time and again, the Bible instructs us to live by faith. Yet despite our best intentions, difficult people and the negative feelings they engender can rob us of the peace and abundance that could be ours—and should be ours—through Christ. When anger, frustration, impatience, or anxiety separate us from the spiritual blessings that God has in store, we must rethink our priorities. And we must place faith above feelings.

Sometimes, amid the inevitable hustle and bustle of daily living, you may lose sight of the real joys of life as you wrestle with the challenges that confront you. Yet joy is available to people (like you) who learn to seek it in proper places and in proper ways. The thoughts you think, the actions you take, the prayers you pray, and the people you serve all have a powerful influence on your emotions.

Who is in charge of your emotions? Is it you, or have you formed the unfortunate habit of letting other people or troubling situations determine the quality of your thoughts and the direction of your day? If you're wise—and if you'd like to build a better life for yourself and your loved ones—you'll learn to control your emotions before your emotions control you.

So the next time you feel your emotions beginning to fray, take a deep breath, step back from the situation, and collect your thoughts. Then ask yourself if the emotions you're feeling are healthy and productive or harmful and destructive. The answer to that question will help you regain control of your thoughts, your emotions, and your life.

MORE THOUGHTS ABOUT YOUR EMOTIONS

Our emotions can lie to us, and we need to counter our emotions with truth.
BILLY GRAHAM

Our feelings do not affect God's facts.
AMY CARMICHAEL

A life lived in God is not lived on the plane of feelings, but of the will.
ELISABETH ELLIOT

If you desire to improve your physical well-being and your emotional outlook, increasing your faith can help you.
JOHN MAXWELL

MORE FROM GOD'S WORD

*All bitterness, anger and wrath, shouting and slander
must be removed from you, along with all malice.
And be kind and compassionate to one another,
forgiving one another, just as God also forgave you in Christ.*
EPHESIANS 4:31–32 HCSB

*Enthusiasm without knowledge is not good.
If you act too quickly, you might make a mistake.*
PROVERBS 19:2 NCV

*And let the peace of God rule in your hearts,
to which also you were called in one body; and be thankful.*
COLOSSIANS 3:15 NKJV

*For this very reason, make every effort
to supplement your faith with goodness,
goodness with knowledge, knowledge with self-control,
self-control with endurance, endurance with godliness.*
2 PETER 1:5–6 HCSB

A TIMELY TIP

Are you sometimes overly emotional? If so, here are the facts: God's
love is real; His peace is real; His support is real. Don't ever let your
emotions obscure these facts. And when you encounter difficult
people or troubling circumstances, step back, say a silent prayer,
and let God handle the things you can't.

59

MANAGING YOUR MENTAL HEALTH

MENTAL HEALTH PROFESSIONALS OFFER HELP

A cheerful disposition is good for your health;
gloom and doom leave you bone-tired.
PROVERBS 17:22 MSG

Although research has clearly proven that many forms of mental illness have physiological causes, far too many people still avoid medical treatment. Instead of seeking help from counselors and physicians, they avoid professional assistance. This failure to seek treatment has consequences that can be unfortunate and, at times, tragic.

So why do so many people avoid the services that mental health professionals can provide? For many sufferers and their families, emotional disorders are still a source of confusion, embarrassment, or shame. Thankfully, the unwarranted stigma of mental illness is fading fast as more and more people come to understand that proven treatments can be life-altering and, in severe cases, life-saving.

Today, mental health is no longer a topic that is spoken about in whispers. Instead, an informed public has become keenly aware that most mental disorders have both medical and psychological origins. Consequently, most emotional disorders, including anxiety disorders, are now eminently treatable through counseling, through medication, or through a combination of the two. So if you suspect that you—or someone you care about—may be suffering from an anxiety disorder or any other psychiatric condition, seek help immediately. By seeking treatment, you'll be managing your *mental* health, which can sometimes be even more important than managing your *physical* health.

To fully experience the joys and celebrations of the Christian life, you need to be spiritually and emotionally healthy. If mental health professionals can help you experience those joys—if they can help you experience God's abundance while you're following in the footsteps of His Son—then you should consider your treatment to be an integral part of the Lord's plan for your life.

MORE THOUGHTS ABOUT MENTAL HEALTH

It's been taboo for so long to admit you have a mental health problem. That must change.

ROSALYNN CARTER

Anything that's human is mentionable, and anything that is mentionable can be more manageable. When we can talk about our feelings, they become less overwhelming, less upsetting, and less scary.

FRED ROGERS

A diagnosis is burden enough without being burdened by secrecy and shame.

JANE PAULEY

More from God's Word

A happy heart makes the face cheerful,
but heartache crushes the spirit.
PROVERBS 15:13 NIV

I have spoken these things to you so that My joy
may be in you and your joy may be complete.
JOHN 15:11 HCSB

O God, restore us and cause Your face
to shine upon us, and we will be saved.
PSALM 80:3 NASB

I urge you to live a life worthy
of the calling you have received.
EPHESIANS 4:1 NIV

And so, dear brothers and sisters,
I plead with you to give your bodies to God. . . .
Let them be a living and holy sacrifice—
the kind he will find acceptable.
This is truly the way to worship him.
ROMANS 12:1 NLT

A Timely Tip

Fitness is a state of body and a state of mind. If you're wise, you'll attend carefully to both.

60

MEDIA

HANDLE THE MEDIA WITH CARE

*Therefore, whether you eat or drink,
or whatever you do, do everything for God's glory.*
1 CORINTHIANS 10:31 HCSB

The Bible assures us that God is always with us, which means that we can live courageously. But sometimes, here in the world of lightning-fast news cycles, it's hard to fight the fearmongers. After all, we face an avalanche of negativity from a widening array of media sources that have discovered bad news sells better than good. So anxiety-producing headlines shout about shocking stories while good news often goes unreported.

The media is working around the clock to grab your attention in an attempt to rearrange your priorities. Yet the all-important things in life have little to do with the alarming images that are so common in today's media-driven world. The most important things in your life have to do with your faith, your family, and your future. Period. So here's a question for you: Will you focus on God's messages or the media's messages? The answer should be obvious.

Perhaps you, like so many others, have experienced anxieties and fears that are fed by the twenty-four-hour news cycle or by gratuitous violence that invades your screen when you least expect it. If so, God wants to remind you that He is here, that He is strong, and that He loves you very much. So don't focus on your fears (or, for that matter, on the fears that big media wants you to focus on). Instead, take your fears to the Lord, and leave them there.

MORE THOUGHTS ABOUT THE MEDIA

Even the briefest look at television and magazine advertising reveals how strongly our culture reinforces attachment to things other than God.
GERALD MAY, MD

The media relentlessly proclaim bad news: for breakfast, lunch, and dinner. A steady diet of their fare will sicken you. Instead of focusing on fickle, ever-changing news broadcasts, tune in to the living Word.
SARAH YOUNG

Reading news without reading the Bible will inevitably lead to an unbalanced life, an anxious spirit, a worried and depressed soul.
BILL BRIGHT

Television is like a thief. It steals time; it kills initiative; it destroys relationships.
EDWIN LOUIS COLE

The Christian life isn't a playground but a battlefield.
BILLY GRAHAM

More from God's Word

*Your adversary, the devil, prowls around
like a roaring lion, seeking someone to devour.*
1 PETER 5:8 NASB

*Put on the whole armor of God, that you may
be able to stand against the wiles of the devil.*
EPHESIANS 6:11 NKJV

*Let us lay aside every weight, and the sin
which so easily ensnares us, and let us run
with endurance the race that is set before us.*
HEBREWS 12:1 NKJV

*No temptation has overtaken you but
such as is common to man; and God is faithful,
who will not allow you to be tempted
beyond what you are able, but with
the temptation will provide the way of escape.*
1 CORINTHIANS 10:13 NASB

A Timely Tip

The world is filled with distractions that can grab your attention and cause you to forget about God. Your job is to focus on God, not the world. And while you're at it, be a discerning viewer. There are a few TV shows worth watching, but there are many more that aren't worth the time it takes to view them. So be careful what you watch.

61

MIRACLES

EXPECT A MIRACLE

Is anything too hard for the LORD?
GENESIS 18:14 NKJV

Do you believe in an all-powerful God who can do miraculous things in you and through you? You should. But perhaps, as you have faced the inevitable struggles of life here on earth, you have—without realizing it—placed limitations on God. To do so is a profound mistake. God's power has no such limitations, and He can work mighty miracles in your own life if you let Him.

Do you lack a firm faith in God's power to perform miracles for you and your loved ones? Have you convinced yourself that your situation is hopeless? If so, you are attempting to place limitations on a God who has none. So instead of doubting your heavenly Father, you must place yourself in His hands. Instead of increasing your anxieties by doubting His power, you must increase your courage by trusting Him. Instead of focusing on your fears and expecting the worst, you must remember that the Lord works miracles.

With God, absolutely nothing is impossible, including an amazing assortment of miracles that He stands ready, willing, and perfectly able to perform for you and yours.

More Thoughts about God's Power to Work Miracles

God specializes in things thought impossible.
CATHERINE MARSHALL

*Faith means believing in realities
that go beyond sense and sight.
It is the awareness of unseen
divine realities all around you.*
JONI EARECKSON TADA

*God's faithfulness and grace
make the impossible possible.*
SHEILA WALSH

*It is wonderful what miracles
God works in wills that are
utterly surrendered to Him.*
HANNAH WHITALL SMITH

Expectation sets the atmosphere for miracles.
A. B. SIMPSON

God is able to do what we can't do.
BILLY GRAHAM

More from God's Word

For with God nothing shall be impossible.
LUKE 1:37 KJV

What no eye has seen, what no ear has heard,
and what no human mind has conceived"—
the things God has prepared for those who love him.
1 CORINTHIANS 2:9 NIV

You are the God of great wonders!
You demonstrate your awesome power among the nations.
PSALM 77:14 NLT

And Jesus looking upon them saith,
With men it is impossible, but not with God:
for with God all things are possible.
MARK 10:27 KJV

And God confirmed the message
by giving signs and wonders and various miracles
and gifts of the Holy Spirit whenever he chose.
HEBREWS 2:4 NLT

A Timely Tip

Nothing is impossible for God. And He's in the business of doing miraculous things. So never be afraid to ask—or to pray—for a miracle.

62

NEGATIVITY

SAY NO TO NEGATIVITY

In my distress I prayed to the LORD,
and the LORD answered me and set me free.
PSALM 118:5 NLT

From experience, we know that it is easier to criticize than to correct; we understand that it is easier to find faults than solutions; and we realize that excessive criticism is usually destructive, not productive. Yet the urge to criticize others remains a powerful temptation for most of us. Our task, as obedient believers, is to break the twin habits of negative thinking and critical speech.

In the book of James, we are issued a clear warning: "Don't criticize one another, brothers" (4:11 HCSB). Undoubtedly, James understood the paralyzing power of chronic negativity, and so must we. Negativity is highly contagious: we give it to others who, in turn, give it back to us. Thankfully, this cycle can be broken by positive thoughts, heartfelt prayers, and encouraging words.

As you examine the quality of your own communications, can you honestly say that you're a booster, not a critic? If so, keep up the good words. But if you're occasionally overwhelmed by negativity, and if you pass that negativity along to your neighbors, it's time for a mental housecleaning and verbal makeover. As a thoughtful Christian, you can use the transforming power of Christ's love to break the chains of negativity. And you should.

MORE THOUGHTS ABOUT MAINTAINING A POSITIVE ATTITUDE

Developing a positive attitude means working continually to find what is uplifting and encouraging.
BARBARA JOHNSON

The things we think are the things that feed our souls. If we think on pure and lovely things, we shall grow pure and lovely like them; and the converse is equally true.
HANNAH WHITALL SMITH

God never promises to remove us from our struggles. He does promise, however, to change the way we look at them.
MAX LUCADO

Have a sincere desire to serve God and mankind, and stop doubting. Stop thinking negatively. Simply start living by faith, pray earnestly and humbly, and get into the habit of looking expectantly for the best.
NORMAN VINCENT PEALE

We choose what attitudes we have right now. And it's a continuing choice.
JOHN MAXWELL

More from God's Word

I say to myself, "The Lord is mine, so I hope in him."
Lamentations 3:24 NCV

*The Lord is good to those who wait for Him,
to the soul who seeks Him. It is good
that one should hope and wait quietly
for the salvation of the Lord.*
Lamentations 3:25–26 NKJV

Hope deferred makes the heart sick.
Proverbs 13:12 NKJV

*Be strong and courageous,
all you who put your hope in the Lord.*
Psalm 31:24 HCSB

Make me to hear joy and gladness.
Psalm 51:8 KJV

A Timely Tip

If your inner voice is like a broken record that keeps repeating negative thoughts, you must guard your heart by training yourself to think thoughts that are more rational, more positive, more forgiving, and less destructive. Remember that negative thinking breeds more negative thinking, so nip negativity in the bud, starting today and continuing every day of your life.

63

OPTIMISM

BE OPTIMISTIC!

We have this hope as an anchor for the soul, sure and strong.
It enters behind the curtain in the Most Holy Place in heaven.
HEBREWS 6:19 NCV

Are you a passionate Christian who expects God to do big things in your life and in the lives of those around you? If you're a thinking Christian, you have every reason to be confident about your future here on earth and your eternal future in heaven. As English clergyman William Ralph Inge observed, "No Christian should be a pessimist, for Christianity is a system of radical optimism." Inge's observation is true, of course, but sometimes you may find yourself caught up in the inevitable complications of everyday living. When you find yourself fretting about the inevitable ups and downs of life here on earth, it's time to slow down, collect yourself, refocus your thoughts, and count your blessings.

God has made promises to you, and He will most certainly keep every one of them. So you have every reason to be an optimist and no legitimate reason to ever abandon hope.

Today, trust your hopes, not your fears. And while you're at it, take time to celebrate God's blessings. His gifts are too numerous to calculate and too glorious to imagine. But it never hurts to try.

More Thoughts about Optimism

*The essence of optimism is that it takes
no account of the present. It is a source
of vitality and hope where others have resigned.
It enables a man to hold his head high,
to claim the future for himself,
and not to abandon it to his enemy.*
Dietrich Bonhoeffer

*Take courage. We walk in the wilderness
today and in the Promised Land tomorrow.*
D. L. Moody

All things work together for good. Fret not, nor fear!
Lettie Cowman

*Come up from the lowlands;
there are heights yet to climb. You cannot
do healthful thinking in the lowlands.
Look to the mountaintop for faith.*
Mary McLeod Bethune

*Avoid arguments, but when a negative
attitude is expressed, counter it
with a positive and optimistic opinion.*
Norman Vincent Peale

More from God's Word

The LORD is my light and my salvation—
whom should I fear? The LORD is the stronghold of my life—
of whom should I be afraid?
PSALM 27:1 HCSB

But if we look forward to something we don't
yet have, we must wait patiently and confidently.
ROMANS 8:25 NLT

Set your mind on things above,
not on things on the earth.
COLOSSIANS 3:2 NKJV

The peace of God, which surpasses
all understanding, will guard your hearts
and minds through Christ Jesus.
PHILIPPIANS 4:7 NKJV

Let us hold on to the confession
of our hope without wavering,
for He who promised is faithful.
HEBREWS 10:23 HCSB

A Timely Tip

As a follower of Christ, you have every reason to be optimistic about your future here on earth and your future in heaven. God is good, and your eternal future is secure, so why not be an optimist?

64

PANIC

DON'T PANIC!

So we can say with confidence,
"The Lord is my helper, so I will have no fear.
What can mere people do to me?"
HEBREWS 13:6 NLT

If you've ever experienced a full-blown panic attack, you can attest to the fact that it is a terrifying experience. Your heart beats faster; you can't catch your breath; your emotions are screaming and you feel frightened beyond words, yet your mind tells you there's nothing to be afraid of. To make matters worse, after you've experienced your first attack, you may develop an ongoing fear of having another one.

Panic attacks occur when we experience an exaggerated physical response to a situation that isn't all that threatening. Researchers aren't completely clear what causes panic attacks, but they can confirm that these are physiological events that include dramatic increases in both heart rate and adrenaline levels. Fortunately, these attacks are highly treatable with counseling, medicine, or both.

So if you've found yourself paralyzed by fear without good reason, don't suffer in silence. Instead, talk to your doctor—or to a

trained mental-help professional who specializes in panic disorders—
and develop a recovery plan. God wants you to experience His joyful abundance, but untreated panic disorders can get in the way. So
don't be afraid or embarrassed to ask for help. It's the surest way to
say no to panic and yes to peace.

MORE THOUGHTS ABOUT PANIC

*Even in the winter, even in the midst of the storm, the sun
is still there. Somewhere, up above the clouds, it still shines
and warms and pulls at the life buried deep inside the brown
branches and frozen earth. The sun is there! Spring will come.*
GLORIA GAITHER

*The fierce grip of panic need not immobilize you.
God knows no limitation when it comes to deliverance.
Admit your fear. Commit it to Him.
Dump the pressure on Him. He can handle it.*
CHARLES SWINDOLL

*Are you weak? Weary? Confused? Troubled? Pressured?
How is your relationship with God? Is it held
in its place of priority? I believe the greater the pressure,
the greater your need for time alone with Him.*
KAY ARTHUR

*Every misfortune, every failure, every loss
may be transformed. God has the power
to transform all misfortunes into "God-sends."*
LETTIE COWMAN

MORE FROM GOD'S WORD

Peace I leave with you; My peace I give to you;
not as the world gives do I give to you.
Do not let your heart be troubled, nor let it be fearful.
JOHN 14:27 NASB

He said to them, "It is I; do not be afraid."
JOHN 6:20 NKJV

Fear not, for I am with you; be not dismayed,
for I am your God. I will strengthen you, yes, I will help you,
I will uphold you with My righteous right hand.
ISAIAH 41:10 NKJV

The LORD is my light and my salvation—
whom should I fear? The LORD is the stronghold
of my life—of whom should I be afraid?
PSALM 27:1 HCSB

Even though I walk through the darkest valley,
I will fear no evil, for you are with me;
your rod and your staff, they comfort me.
PSALM 23:4 NIV

A TIMELY TIP

If you experience a full-blown panic attack, don't try to handle it on your own. Instead, talk to your physician. Medical professionals and knowledgeable counselors can offer solutions, but they won't offer them to you unless they're asked.

65

PEACE

EXPERIENCING GOD'S PEACE

These things I have spoken to you, that in Me
you may have peace. In the world you will have tribulation;
but be of good cheer, I have overcome the world.

JOHN 16:33 NKJV

Have you found the lasting peace that can—and should—be yours through Jesus Christ? Or are you still chasing the illusion of "peace and happiness" that the world promises but cannot deliver?

The Scottish preacher George McDonald observed, "It has been well said that no man ever sank under the burden of the day. It is when tomorrow's burden is added to the burden of today that the weight is more than a man can bear. Never load yourselves so, my friends. If you find yourselves so loaded, at least remember this: it is your own doing, not God's. He begs you to leave the future to Him."

Today, as a gift to yourself, to your family, and to your friends, claim the inner peace that is your spiritual birthright: the peace of Jesus Christ. Christ is standing at the door, waiting patiently for you to invite Him to reign in your heart. His eternal peace is offered freely. Claim it today.

MORE THOUGHTS ABOUT EXPERIENCING GOD'S PEACE

When something robs you of your peace of mind,
ask yourself if it is worth the energy you are expending on it.
If not, then put it out of your mind in an act of discipline.
Every time the thought of "it" returns, refuse it.

KAY ARTHUR

Peace does not mean to be in a place where there is no noise,
trouble, or hard work. Peace means to be in the midst of all
those things and still be calm in your heart.

CATHERINE MARSHALL

In the center of a hurricane there is absolute quiet and peace.
There is no safer place than in the center of the will of God.

CORRIE TEN BOOM

Deep within the center of the soul is a chamber of peace
where God lives and where, if we will enter it and quiet
all the other sounds, we can hear His gentle whisper.

LETTIE COWMAN

God's power is great enough for our deepest desperation.
You can go on. You can pick up the pieces and start anew.
You can face your fears. You can find peace in the rubble.
There is healing for your soul.

SUZANNE DALE EZELL

More from God's Word

He Himself is our peace.
EPHESIANS 2:14 NASB

*"I will give peace, real peace, to those far and near,
and I will heal them," says the LORD.*
ISAIAH 57:19 NCV

*But the fruit of the Spirit is love, joy, peace,
patience, kindness, goodness, faith, gentleness, self-control.
Against such things there is no law.*
GALATIANS 5:22–23 HCSB

*The peace of God, which passeth all understanding,
shall keep your hearts and minds through Christ Jesus.*
PHILIPPIANS 4:7 KJV

*Peace I leave with you, My peace I give to you;
not as the world gives do I give to you. Let not your
heart be troubled, neither let it be afraid.*
JOHN 14:27 NKJV

A Timely Tip

Sometimes peace can be a scarce commodity in this noisy, complicated world. But God's peace is always available when you turn everything over to Him. The Lord is ready to calm your fears, renew your strength, and give you peace of mind *if* you let Him. The rest is up to you.

66

PEER PRESSURE

SAYING NO TO
NEGATIVE PEER PRESSURE

*Do not be mismatched with unbelievers. For what
partnership is there between righteousness and lawlessness?
Or what fellowship does light have with darkness?*
2 CORINTHIANS 6:14 HCSB

Peer pressure can be a good thing or a bad thing, depending upon
your peers. If your peers encourage you to make integrity a habit—
and if they encourage you to follow God's will and to obey His
commandments—then you'll experience positive peer pressure, and
that's good. But if you are involved with people who encourage you
to do foolish things, you're facing a different kind of peer pressure:
the negative kind. And the more negative peer pressure you experience, the more anxious you'll become.

Rick Warren observed, "Those who follow the crowd usually
get lost in it." We know those words to be true, but oftentimes
we fail to live by them. Instead of trusting God for guidance, we
imitate our friends and suffer the consequences. Instead of seeking
to please our Father in heaven, we strive to please our peers, with
decidedly mixed results. Instead of doing the right thing, we do the

"easy" thing or the "popular" thing. And when we do, we pay a high price for our shortsightedness.

Would you like a time-tested formula for successful living? Here is a simple formula that is proven and true: don't give in to negative peer pressure. Period. Instead of getting lost in the crowd, seek guidance from God. Does this sound too simple? Perhaps it is simple, but it is also the only way to reap all the marvelous riches that the Lord has in store for you.

MORE THOUGHTS ABOUT PEER PRESSURE

Character is always lost when a high ideal is sacrificed on the altar of conformity and popularity.
CHARLES SWINDOLL

Many Christians give in to various temptations through peer pressure. They find themselves surrendering to worldly passions, justifying pleasures the world offers.
BILLY GRAHAM

Fashion is an enduring testimony to the fact that we live quite consciously before the eyes of others.
JOHN ELDREDGE

I don't know all the keys to success, but one key to failure is to try to please everyone.
RICK WARREN

More from God's Word

My son, if sinners entice you, don't be persuaded.
PROVERBS 1:10 HCSB

Dear friend, do not imitate what is evil,
but what is good. The one who does good is of God;
the one who does evil has not seen God.
3 JOHN 1:11 HCSB

No, God is the One I am trying to please.
Am I trying to please people? If I still wanted
to please people, I would not be a servant of Christ.
GALATIANS 1:10 NCV

Peter and the apostles replied,
"We must obey God rather than men."
ACTS 5:29 HCSB

Do not be deceived: "Bad company corrupts good morals."
1 CORINTHIANS 15:33 HCSB

A Timely Tip

Peer pressure can be good or bad. God wants you to seek out the good and flee from the bad. So if you encounter someone who encourages you to behave badly—or to betray your conscience—run, don't walk, in the opposite direction.

67

PERFECTIONISM

BEYOND PERFECTIONISM

Those who wait for perfect weather will never plant seeds;
those who look at every cloud will never harvest crops. . . .
Plant early in the morning, and work until evening, because you
don't know if this or that will succeed. They might both do well.
ECCLESIASTES 11:4,6 NCV

As a citizen of the twenty-first century, you know that demands can be high, and expectations even higher. Traditional media outlets, along with their social-media counterparts, deliver an endless stream of messages that tell you how to look, how to behave, how to eat, and how to dress. And that's only the beginning. If you're not careful, you'll find yourself scrambling to keep up with everybody's expectations, which is impossible.

The world's expectations are impossible to meet—God's are not. God doesn't expect you to be perfect, and neither, by the way, should you. So if you're a person who possesses perfectionistic tendencies, here's a word of warning: perfectionism and anxiety are traveling companions. If you're striving to be perfect, you'll inevitably make yourself more anxious than necessary. To combat perfectionism, remember this: the expectations that really matter are God's expectations. Everything else takes a back seat.

So do your best to please God, and don't worry too much about what other people think. And when it comes to meeting the unrealistic expectations of a world gone haywire, forget about trying to be perfect—it's impossible.

MORE THOUGHTS ABOUT PERFECTIONISM

God is so inconceivably good. He's not looking for perfection. He already saw it in Christ. He's looking for affection.
BETH MOORE

The happiest people in the world are not those who have no problems, but the people who have learned to live with those things that are less than perfect.
JAMES DOBSON

The greatest destroyer of good works is the desire to do great works.
C. H. SPURGEON

We shall never come to the perfect man till we come to the perfect world.
MATTHEW HENRY

What makes a Christian a Christian is not perfection but forgiveness.
MAX LUCADO

MORE FROM GOD'S WORD

Let not your heart be troubled;
you believe in God, believe also in Me.
JOHN 14:1 NKJV

In thee, O LORD, do I put my trust;
let me never be put to confusion.
PSALM 71:1 KJV

The fear of human opinion disables;
trusting in God protects you from that.
PROVERBS 29:25 MSG

For everything created by God is good, and nothing
is to be rejected if it is received with gratitude.
1 TIMOTHY 4:4 NASB

Your beliefs about these things should be kept secret
between you and God. People are happy if they can
do what they think is right without feeling guilty.
ROMANS 14:22 NCV

A TIMELY TIP

In heaven, we will know perfection. Here on earth, we have a few short years to wrestle with the challenges of imperfection. God is perfect; we human beings are not. May we live—and forgive—accordingly.

68

PERSEVERANCE

THE POWER OF PERSEVERANCE

*Let us not become weary in doing good, for at the proper
time we will reap a harvest if we do not give up.*
GALATIANS 6:9 NIV

If you're trying to rid yourself of anxious thoughts or unfounded
fears, you will undoubtedly experience a few setbacks along the way.
When you do, don't be discouraged. Instead, keep searching for
more effective ways to manage your negative emotions. And while
you're at it, remember that God isn't finished with you yet.

The old saying is as true today as it was when it was first spoken:
"Life is a marathon, not a sprint." That's why wise travelers (like
you) select a traveling companion who never tires and never falters.
That partner, of course, is your heavenly Father.

The next time you find your courage tested by anxious thoughts
or unfortunate circumstances, remember that God is as near as your
next breath, and remember that He offers strength and comfort
to His children. He is your shield and your strength; He is your
protector and your deliverer. Call upon Him in your hour of need
and be comforted. Whatever your challenge, whatever your trouble,
God can help you persevere. And that's precisely what He'll do if

you ask Him. Whatever your problem, God can handle it. Your job is to keep persevering until He does.

MORE THOUGHTS ABOUT PERSEVERANCE

Patience and diligence, like faith, remove mountains.
WILLIAM PENN

Everyone gets discouraged. The question is:
Are you going to give up or get up? It's a choice.
JOHN MAXWELL

Perseverance is not a passive submission
to circumstances—it is a strong and active
response to the difficult events of life.
ELIZABETH GEORGE

Perseverance is more than endurance. It is endurance
combined with absolute assurance and certainty
that what we are looking for is going to happen.
OSWALD CHAMBERS

You may have to fight a battle more than once to win it.
MARGARET THATCHER

Character consists of what you do
on the third and fourth tries.
JAMES MICHENER

MORE FROM GOD'S WORD

So let us run the race that is before us and never give up.
We should remove from our lives anything that would
get in the way and the sin that so easily holds us back.
HEBREWS 12:1 NCV

We are hard-pressed on every side, yet not crushed;
we are perplexed, but not in despair.
2 CORINTHIANS 4:8 NKJV

For you have need of endurance, so that when you have
done the will of God, you may receive what was promised.
HEBREWS 10:36 NASB

Finishing is better than starting.
Patience is better than pride.
ECCLESIASTES 7:8 NLT

But as for you, be strong; don't be discouraged,
for your work has a reward.
2 CHRONICLES 15:7 HCSB

A TIMELY TIP

When you're experiencing anxious thoughts or unfounded fears, you may be tempted to give in to negativity and doubt. Resist the temptation. When you are tested, don't quit at the first sign of trouble. Instead, call upon God. He can give you the strength to persevere, and that's exactly what you should ask Him to do.

69

PESSIMISM

SAY NO TO PESSIMISM

The LORD is my light and my salvation; whom shall I fear?
The LORD is the strength of my life; of whom shall I be afraid?
PSALM 27:1 NKJV

Pessimism is emotional poison. And negativity has the power to harm your heart if you let it. So if you've allowed negative thoughts to creep into your mind and heart, here's your assignment: start spending more time thinking about your blessings and less time fretting about your hardships.

God has promised to protect us, and He intends to fulfill His promise. In a world filled with dangers and temptations, God is the ultimate armor. In a world filled with misleading messages, God's Word is the ultimate truth.

This day, like every other, is a gift from above, filled to the brim with possibilities. But persistent pessimistic thoughts can rob you of the energy you need to accomplish the most important tasks on your to-do list. So today, be careful to direct your thoughts toward things positive. And while you're at it, take time to thank the Giver of all things good for gifts that are, in truth, far too numerous to count.

MORE THOUGHTS ABOUT REPLACING PESSIMISM WITH OPTIMISM

Occupy your minds with good thoughts, or your enemy will fill them with bad ones; unoccupied they cannot be.
ST. THOMAS MORE

Two types of voices command your attention today. Negative ones fill your mind with doubt, bitterness, and fear. Positive ones purvey hope and strength. Which one will you choose to heed?
MAX LUCADO

Developing a positive attitude means working continually to find what is uplifting and encouraging.
BARBARA JOHNSON

Never yield to gloomy anticipation. Place your hope and confidence in God. He has no record of failure.
LETTIE COWMAN

Find the good. It's all around you. Find it, showcase it, and you'll start believing in it.
JESSE OWENS

After one hour in heaven, we shall be ashamed that we ever grumbled.
VANCE HAVNER

More from God's Word

Let us hold fast the confession of
our hope without wavering,
for He who promised is faithful.
HEBREWS 10:23 NASB

Make me to hear joy and gladness.
PSALM 51:8 KJV

But if we look forward to something we don't yet have,
we must wait patiently and confidently.
ROMANS 8:25 NLT

Let us not become weary in doing good,
for at the proper time we will reap
a harvest if we do not give up.
GALATIANS 6:9 NIV

But as for you, be strong; don't be discouraged,
for your work has a reward.
2 CHRONICLES 15:7 HCSB

A Timely Tip

Negative self-talk breeds negative results. Positive self-talk breeds positive results. So as you monitor your thoughts, stay positive. And whatever you do, please don't let chronic negativity shape your future.

70

POSSIBILITIES

YES, YOU CAN LEARN
TO CONTROL YOUR EMOTIONS

I can do all things through Christ which strengtheneth me.
PHILIPPIANS 4:13 KJV

All of us face difficult days, days when then challenges of everyday life threaten to hijack our emotions. Sometimes even the most optimistic Christians can become discouraged, and you are no exception. If you find yourself enduring difficult circumstances, perhaps it's time for an extreme intellectual makeover; perhaps it's time to focus more on your strengths and opportunities and less on the challenges that confront you.

If you believe, even for a moment, that you can never learn to deal with anxiety and fear, you are mistaken. With God, all things are possible. So keep praying, keep thinking good thoughts, and don't be embarrassed to talk with a trained mental health professional if necessary. And while you're at it, keep reminding yourself that better days are ahead.

Every day, including this one, is brimming with possibilities. Every day is filled with opportunities to heal, to grow, to serve, to share, and to rise above unfortunate situations. But if you are entangled in a web of anxious thoughts, you may overlook the blessings that God has scattered along your path. So don't give in to pessimism, to doubt, to cynicism, or to fear. Instead, keep your eyes focused upon the possibilities, fix your heart upon the Creator, do your best, and let Him handle the rest.

MORE THOUGHTS ABOUT POSSIBILITIES

Do not limit the limitless God! With Him,
face the future unafraid because you are never alone.
LETTIE COWMAN

Beware in your prayers, above everything else,
of limiting God, not only by unbelief, but by fancying
that you know what He can do. Expect unexpected things.
ANDREW MURRAY

We are all faced with a series of great opportunities
brilliantly disguised as impossible situations.
CHARLES SWINDOLL

Eliminate the word "impossible" from your conversation;
drop it from your thoughts; erase it from your attitudes.
Substitute for it that bright and shining word "possible."
NORMAN VINCENT PEALE

God's specialty is raising dead things to life
and making impossible things possible.
You don't have the need that exceeds His power.
BETH MOORE

More from God's Word

Is anything too hard for the LORD?
GENESIS 18:14 KJV

Jesus said to him, "If you can believe,
all things are possible to him who believes."
MARK 9:23 NKJV

Therefore we do not lose heart.
Even though our outward man is perishing,
yet the inward man is being renewed day by day.
2 CORINTHIANS 4:16 NKJV

The things which are impossible
with men are possible with God.
LUKE 18:27 KJV

But Jesus looked at them and said to them,
"With men this is impossible,
but with God all things are possible."
MATTHEW 19:26 NKJV

A Timely Tip

Dealing with anxious thoughts and roller-coaster emotions can be painful, but with God's help you're up to the challenge. Keep praying and keep trying to do the right thing. And remember: with God, all things are possible.

71

POST-TRAUMATIC STRESS

TREATMENT FOR PTSD
IS AVAILABLE AND ESSENTIAL

Blessed are those who mourn, for they shall be comforted.
MATTHEW 5:4 NKJV

Post-traumatic stress disorder (PTSD) is an anxiety disorder that occurs after a highly stressful, deeply disturbing event. People who suffer from PTSD may have insomnia, flashbacks, low self-esteem, and a host of other unpleasant symptoms. They may also experience emotional numbing, hypervigilance, and suicidal thoughts. So it's clear that PTSD is a serious psychological and medical condition that should be treated by trained counselors and medical professionals.

Response to trauma is a highly individualized experience: what's traumatic to one person may not be to another. That being said, there are still certain experiences that make PTSD more likely. People who experience war, assault, a serious accident, or a natural disaster are obviously at risk. Generally speaking, women are at greater risk of PTSD than men.

If you or someone you love has experienced a traumatic event, don't hesitate to ask for help. It's better to seek help and recover than to "tough it out" and suffer. God wants you and your loved ones to experience His abundance. Now.

MORE THOUGHTS ABOUT PTSD

When frustrations develop into problems that
stress you out, the best way to cope is to stop,
catch your breath, and do something for yourself,
not out of selfishness, but out of wisdom.
BARBARA JOHNSON

Stress is as necessary to fine-tuning in life
as it is to fine-tuning a guitar string.
EDWIN LOUIS COLE

The creation of a new heart, the renewing
of a right spirit is an omnipotent work of God.
Leave it to the Creator.
HENRY DRUMMOND

Life is strenuous. See that your clock does not run down.
LETTIE COWMAN

Beware of having so much to do
that you really do nothing at all because
you do not wait upon God to do it aright.
C. H. SPURGEON

More from God's Word

Come unto me, all ye that labor and are heavy laden,
and I will give you rest.
MATTHEW 11:28 KJV

And the peace of God, which transcends all understanding,
will guard your hearts and your minds in Christ Jesus.
PHILIPPIANS 4:7 NIV

I find rest in God; only he gives me hope.
PSALM 62:5 NCV

Peace I leave with you; My peace I give to you;
not as the world gives do I give to you.
Do not let your heart be troubled, nor let it be fearful.
JOHN 14:27 NASB

You, LORD, give true peace to those who
depend on you, because they trust you.
ISAIAH 26:3 NCV

A Timely Tip

If you suspect that you, or someone you care about, may be suffering from PTSD, please seek professional help immediately. PTSD can be treated with medications or psychotherapy or both. Help is available. Ask for it today.

72

PRAYING ABOUT YOUR ANXIETIES

Therefore I say to you, whatever things you ask when you pray,
believe that you receive them, and you will have them.
MARK 11:24 NKJV

Want an easy-to-use, highly reliable, readily available antidote to anxiety and stress? Well here it is: it's called prayer.

Is prayer an integral part of your daily life, or is it a hit-or-miss habit? Do you "pray without ceasing," or is your prayer life an afterthought? Do you regularly pray in the solitude of the early morning darkness, or do you lower your head only when others are watching? The answer to these questions will determine both the direction of your day and the way that you deal with the inevitable stressors of everyday life.

So instead of trying to do everything on your own, form the habit of asking God for His help. Begin your prayers early in the morning and continue them throughout the day. And remember this: God does answer your prayers, but He's not likely to answer those prayers until you've prayed them.

MORE THOUGHTS ABOUT
THE IMPORTANCE OF PRAYER

Prayer is of transcendent importance. Prayer is the mightiest agent to advance God's work. Praying hearts and hands only can do God's work. Prayer succeeds when all else fails.

E. M. BOUNDS

Time spent in prayer will yield more than that given to work. Prayer alone gives work its worth and its success. Prayer opens the way for God Himself to do His work in us and through us.

ANDREW MURRAY

Before prayer changes others, it first changes us.

BILLY GRAHAM

We should always pray with as much earnestness as those who expect everything from God; we should always act with as much energy as those who expect everything from themselves.

CHARLES COLSON

Any concern that is too small to be turned into a prayer is too small to be made into a burden.

CORRIE TEN BOOM

Prayer should not be merely an act, but an attitude of life.

BILLY GRAHAM

More from God's Word

Rejoice always, pray without ceasing,
in everything give thanks; for this is
the will of God in Christ Jesus for you.
1 Thessalonians 5:16–18 NKJV

Is anyone among you suffering? He should pray.
James 5:13 HCSB

Be joyful because you have hope.
Be patient when trouble comes, and pray at all times.
Romans 12:12 NCV

Ask, and it will be given to you; seek, and you will find;
knock, and it will be opened to you. For everyone
who asks receives, and he who seeks finds,
and to him who knocks it will be opened.
Matthew 7:7–8 NASB

May these words of my mouth and this meditation
of my heart be pleasing in your sight,
Lord, my Rock and my Redeemer.
Psalm 19:14 NIV

A Timely Tip

If you need something, don't ask for God's help in general terms.
Ask specifically for the things you need.

73

PRAYING ABOUT
YOUR FEARS

*In the day of my trouble I shall call upon You,
for You will answer me.*
PSALM 86:7 NASB

Would you like to overcome irrational fears and exaggerated worries? If the answer to that question is yes, then you should set aside ample time for prayer and praise. As Christians, we are instructed to pray often. But it is important to note that genuine prayer requires much more than bending our knees and closing our eyes. Heartfelt prayer is an attitude of the heart.

If your prayers have become more a matter of habit than a matter of passion, you're robbing yourself of a deeper relationship with God. And how can you rectify that situation? By praying more frequently and more fervently. When you do, God will give you the courage and the perspective to deal with your fears.

Too many of us, even well-intentioned believers, tend to "compartmentalize" our waking hours into a few familiar categories: work, rest, play, family time, and worship. To do so is a mistake. Worship and praise should be woven into the fabric of our lives;

prayer should never be relegated to a weekly three-hour visit to church on Sunday morning.

Theologian Wayne Oates once admitted, "Many of my prayers are made with my eyes open. You see, it seems I'm always praying about something, and it's not always convenient—or safe—to close my eyes." Dr. Oates understood that God always hears our prayers and that the relative position of our eyelids is of no concern to Him.

Today, find a little more time to lift your concerns to God in prayer, and praise Him for all that He has done. Whether your eyes are open or closed, He's listening.

MORE THOUGHTS ABOUT PRAYER

Prayer wonderfully clears the vision; steadies the nerves; defines duty; stiffens the purpose; sweetens and strengthens the spirit.
S. D. GORDON

When there is a matter that requires definite prayer, pray until you believe God and until you can thank Him for His answer.
HANNAH WHITALL SMITH

The vigor of our spiritual life will be in exact proportion to the place held by the Bible in our life and thoughts.
GEORGE MUELLER

A prayerful heart and an obedient heart will learn, very slowly and not without sorrow, to stake everything on God Himself.
ELISABETH ELLIOT

More from God's Word

I desire therefore that the men pray everywhere,
lifting up holy hands, without wrath and doubting.
1 Timothy 2:8 NKJV

Then if my people who are called by my name will
humble themselves and pray and seek my face and turn
from their wicked ways, I will hear from heaven
and will forgive their sins and restore their land.
2 Chronicles 7:14 NLT

But when you are praying, first forgive anyone
you are holding a grudge against, so that your
Father in heaven will forgive your sins, too.
Mark 11:25 NLT

So I tell you to believe that you have received the things
you ask for in prayer, and God will give them to you.
Mark 11:24 NCV

A Timely Tip

Ask yourself if your prayer life is all that it should be. If the answer is yes, keep up the good work. But if the answer is no, set aside a specific time each morning to talk to God. And then, when you've set aside a time for prayer, don't allow yourself to become sidetracked. Give God your full attention by putting prayer at the very top of your daily to-do list.

74

PRAYING FOR A PEACEFUL HEART

PRAY FOR PEACE OF MIND

*Be anxious for nothing, but in everything by prayer
and supplication, with thanksgiving,
let your requests be made known to God.*
PHILIPPIANS 4:6 NKJV

When you're enduring difficult circumstances, it's easy to become frustrated. But even in the most difficult situations, God offers His peace if you ask for it. The beautiful words of John 14:27 remind us that Jesus offers us peace, not as the world gives, but as He alone gives: "Peace I leave with you. My peace I give to you. I do not give to you as the world gives. Your heart must not be troubled or fearful." Our challenge is to accept Christ's peace and then, as best we can, to share His peace with our neighbors.

Today, as a gift to yourself, to your family, and to your friends, claim the inner peace that is your spiritual birthright: the peace of Jesus Christ. It is offered freely; it has been paid for in full; it is yours for the asking. So ask. And then share.

As you go about your daily activities, remember God's instructions:

"Rejoice always! Pray constantly. Give thanks in everything, for this is God's will for you in Christ Jesus" (1 Thessalonians 5:16–18 HCSB). Start praying in the morning and keep praying until you fall off to sleep at night. And rest assured: God is always listening, and He always wants to hear from you.

MORE THOUGHTS ABOUT PRAYING FOR A PEACEFUL HEART

Prayer begins by talking to God,
but it ends in listening to Him.
In the face of Absolute Truth,
silence is the soul's language.
FULTON J. SHEEN

No man is greater than his prayer life.
LEONARD RAVENHILL

You must go forward on your knees.
HUDSON TAYLOR

God's solution is just a prayer away!
MAX LUCADO

Is prayer your steering wheel or your spare tire?
CORRIE TEN BOOM

More from God's Word

These things I have spoken to you, that in Me
you may have peace. In the world you will have tribulation;
but be of good cheer, I have overcome the world.
JOHN 16:33 NKJV

The peace of God, which passeth all understanding,
shall keep your hearts and minds through Christ Jesus.
PHILIPPIANS 4:7 KJV

You, LORD, give true peace to those who
depend on you, because they trust you.
ISAIAH 26:3 NCV

"I will give peace, real peace, to those far and near,
and I will heal them," says the LORD.
ISAIAH 57:19 NCV

He Himself is our peace.
EPHESIANS 2:14 NASB

A Timely Tip

God's peace is available to you this very moment if you place absolute trust in Him. The Lord is your shepherd. Trust Him today and be blessed.

75

PRIORITIES

SETTING THE RIGHT PRIORITIES

Seek first God's kingdom and what God wants.
Then all your other needs will be met as well.
MATTHEW 6:33 NCV

First things first." These words are easy to speak but hard to put into practice. For busy people living in a demanding world, placing first things first can be difficult indeed. Why? Because so many people are expecting so many things from us!

If you're anxiously agonizing over a to-do list that seems impossibly long, perhaps you've been trying to organize your life according to your own plans, not God's. A better strategy, of course, is to take your daily obligations and place them in the hands of the One who created you. To do so, you must prioritize your day according to God's commandments, and you must seek His will and His wisdom in all matters. Then, you can face the day with the assurance that the same God who created our universe out of nothingness will help you place first things first in your own life.

Do you feel overwhelmed, anxious, or emotionally distraught? If so, turn the concerns of this day over to God—prayerfully, earnestly, and often. Then, listen for His answer, and trust the answer He gives.

MORE THOUGHTS ABOUT SETTING THE RIGHT PRIORITIES

*Put first things first and we get second
things thrown in; put second things first
and we lose both first and second things.*

ELIZABETH GEORGE

*A disciple is a follower of Christ.
That means you take on His priorities
as your own. His agenda becomes
your agenda. His mission becomes your mission.*

CHARLES STANLEY

*Great relief and satisfaction can come from seeking God's
priorities for us in each season, discerning what is "best"
in the midst of many noble opportunities, and pouring
our most excellent energies into those things.*

BETH MOORE

*Energy and time are limited entities. Therefore, we need
to use them wisely, focusing on what is truly important.*

SARAH YOUNG

*Each day is God's gift of a fresh unspoiled
opportunity to live according to His priorities.*

ELIZABETH GEORGE

MORE FROM GOD'S WORD

For where your treasure is,
there your heart will be also.
LUKE 12:34 HCSB

Trust in the LORD with all your heart
and lean not on your own understanding.
PROVERBS 3:5 NIV

Prove yourselves doers of the word,
and not merely hearers who delude themselves.
JAMES 1:22 NASB

Make yourself an example of good works
with integrity and dignity in your teaching.
TITUS 2:7 HCSB

Therefore, whether you eat or drink,
or whatever you do, do everything for God's glory.
1 CORINTHIANS 10:31 HCSB

A TIMELY TIP

You don't have time to do everything, so it's perfectly okay to say no to the things that mean less so that you'll have time for the things that matter more.

76

PROBLEM SOLVING

PROBLEM SOLVING 101

People who do what is right may have many problems,
but the LORD will solve them all.
PSALM 34:19 NCV

It's inevitable: the upcoming day will not be problem-free. In fact, your life can be viewed as an exercise in problem solving. The question is not whether you will encounter difficult situations or prickly problems; the real question is how you will choose to respond.

When it comes to solving the problems of everyday living, we often know precisely what needs to be done, but we may be slow in doing it—especially if what needs to be done is difficult or uncomfortable. So we put off till tomorrow what should be done today.

The words of Psalm 34 remind us that the Lord solves problems for "people who do what is right." And usually, doing "what is right" means doing the uncomfortable work of confronting our problems sooner rather than later. So with no further ado, let the problem solving begin *now*.

More Thoughts about Problem Solving

*Every misfortune, every failure, every loss
may be transformed. God has the power
to transform all misfortunes into "God-sends."*
Lettie Cowman

*Faith points us beyond our problems
to the hope we have in Christ.*
Billy Graham

*Human problems are never greater
than divine solutions.*
Erwin Lutzer

Each problem is a God-appointed instructor.
Charles Swindoll

*Everyone gets discouraged.
The question is: Are you going to
give up or get up? It's a choice.*
John Maxwell

*Nine-tenths of the difficulties
are overcome when our hearts
are ready to do the Lord's will.*
George Mueller

MORE FROM GOD'S WORD

We also have joy with our troubles,
because we know that these troubles
produce patience. And patience produces
character, and character produces hope.
ROMANS 5:3–4 NCV

We are pressured in every way but not crushed;
we are perplexed but not in despair.
2 CORINTHIANS 4:8 HCSB

Trust the LORD your God with all your heart and lean not
on your own understanding; in all your ways
submit to him, and he will make your paths straight.
PROVERBS 3:5–6 NIV

Consider it a great joy, my brothers, whenever you experience
various trials, knowing that the testing of your faith produces
endurance. But endurance must do its complete work, so that
you may be mature and complete, lacking nothing.
JAMES 1:2–4 HCSB

A TIMELY TIP

There are two kinds of problems that you should never worry about: the small ones that you can handle and the big ones that God can handle. The problems that are simply too big to solve should be left in God's hands while you invest your energy in things that you do have the power fix.

77

PROCRASTINATION

BEYOND PROCRASTINATION

Prove yourselves doers of the word,
and not merely hearers who delude themselves.
JAMES 1:22 NASB

If you find yourself bound by the chains of procrastination, ask yourself what you're waiting for—or more accurately what you're afraid of—and why. As you examine the emotional roadblocks that have heretofore blocked your path, you may discover that you're waiting for the "perfect" moment, that instant in time when you feel neither afraid nor anxious. But in truth, perfect moments like these are few and far between.

So stop waiting for the perfect moment and focus, instead, on finding the right moment to do what needs to be done. Then trust God and get busy. When you do, you'll discover that you and the Father, working together, can accomplish great things . . . and that you can accomplish them sooner rather than later.

Once you acquire the habit of doing what needs to be done when it needs to be done, you will avoid untold trouble, worry, and stress. So learn to overcome procrastination by paying less attention to your fears and more attention to your responsibilities. God has created a world that punishes procrastinators and rewards people who "do it now." In other words, life doesn't procrastinate. Neither should you.

MORE THOUGHTS ABOUT PROCRASTINATION

Don't wait to "feel" like doing a thing to do it.
Live by decision, not emotion.
JOYCE MEYER

Our grand business is, not to see
what lies dimly at a distance,
but to do what lies closely at hand.
THOMAS CARLYLE

Every duty which we omit obscures some
truth which we should have known.
JOHN RUSKIN

Do noble things, not dream them
all day long; and so make life, death,
and that vast forever one grand, sweet song.
CHARLES KINGSLEY

One today is worth two tomorrows.
BEN FRANKLIN

More from God's Word

*Therefore, get your minds ready for action,
be serious and set your hope completely on the grace
to be brought to you at the revelation of Jesus Christ.*
1 PETER 1:13 HCSB

For the kingdom of God is not in talk but of power.
1 CORINTHIANS 4:20 HCSB

*When you make a vow to God, do not delay to fulfill it.
He has no pleasure in fools; fulfill your vow.*
ECCLESIASTES 5:4 NIV

*People who do what is right may have many problems,
but the LORD will solve them all.*
PSALM 34:19 NCV

I can do all things through Him who strengthens me.
PHILIPPIANS 4:13 NASB

A Timely Tip

The habit of procrastination is often rooted in the fear of failure, the fear of discomfort, or the fear of embarrassment. Your challenge is to confront these fears and defeat them. So if unpleasant work needs to be done, do it sooner rather than later. It's easy to put off unpleasant tasks, but a far better strategy is this: do the unpleasant work first so you can enjoy the rest of the day. The sooner you face your problems—and the sooner you begin working to resolve them—the better your life will be.

78

PUTTING GOD FIRST

ALWAYS PUT GOD FIRST

You shall have no other gods before Me.
EXODUS 20:3 NKJV

For most of us, these are very busy times. We have obligations at home, at work, at school, or at church. From the moment we rise until we drift off to sleep at night, we have things to do and people to contact. So how do we find time for God? We must *make* time for Him, plain and simple. When we put God first, we're blessed. But when we succumb to the pressures and temptations of the world, we inevitably pay a price for our misguided priorities.

In the book of Exodus, God warns that we should put no gods before Him. Yet all too often, we place our Lord in second, third, or fourth place as we focus on other things. When we place our desires for possessions and status above our love for God—or when we yield to the countless frustrations and distractions that surround us—we forfeit the peace that might otherwise be ours.

In the wilderness, Satan offered Jesus earthly power and unimaginable riches, but Jesus refused. Instead, He chose to worship His heavenly Father. We must do likewise by putting God first and worshiping Him only. God must come first. Always first.

MORE THOUGHTS ABOUT PUTTING GOD FIRST

Jesus Christ is the first and last,
author and finisher, beginning and end,
alpha and omega, and by Him
all other things hold together.
He must be first or nothing.
God never comes next!
VANCE HAVNER

The most important thing
you must decide to do every day
is put the Lord first.
ELIZABETH GEORGE

God wants to be in our
leisure time as much as He is
in our churches and in our work.
BETH MOORE

Even the most routine part of your day
can be a spiritual act of worship.
SARAH YOUNG

Christ is either Lord of all,
or He is not Lord at all.
HUDSON TAYLOR

More from God's Word

*Jesus said to him, "You shall love the LORD your God
with all your heart, with all your soul, and with
all your mind." This is the first and great commandment.*
MATTHEW 22:37–38 NKJV

*With my whole heart I have sought You;
oh, let me not wander from Your commandments!*
PSALM 119:10 NKJV

Be careful not to forget the LORD.
DEUTERONOMY 6:12 HCSB

*Do not love the world or the things that belong to the world.
If anyone loves the world, love for the Father is not in him.*
1 JOHN 2:15 HCSB

*No one can serve two masters. For you will hate one
and love the other; you will be devoted to one and despise
the other. You cannot serve God and be enslaved to money.*
LUKE 16:13 NLT

A Timely Tip

God deserves first place in your heart, and you deserve the experience of putting Him there and keeping Him there. So don't let troublesome circumstances or irrational fears monopolize your thoughts. Put God first. When you do, everything else has a way of falling into place.

79

Quiet Time

Finding Strength in Quiet Moments

In quietness and in confidence shall be your strength.
ISAIAH 30:15 KJV

The world seems to grow louder day by day, and angry people are using technology to spread negativity far and wide. No wonder our senses seem to be invaded at every turn. If we allow the inevitable distractions of a clamorous society to separate us from God's peace, we do ourselves a profound disservice.

If we sincerely want the peace that passes all understanding, we must carve out time each day for prayer, reflection, and Bible study. When we meet with God in the morning, we can quiet our minds and sense His presence.

Has the busy pace of life robbed you of the peace that God has promised? If so, it's time to reorder your priorities and rearrange your schedule. Nothing is more important than the time you spend with your heavenly Father. So be still and claim the inner peace that is found in the silent moments you spend with Him.

MORE THOUGHTS ABOUT QUIET TIME

God's voice is still and quiet
and easily buried under
an avalanche of clamor.
CHARLES STANLEY

Strength is found not in busyness
and noise but in quietness.
LETTIE COWMAN

The world is full of noise.
Might we not set ourselves
to learn silence, stillness, solitude?
ELISABETH ELLIOT

Nothing in all creation is so like God as stillness.
JOHANN WOLFGANG VON GOETHE

I don't see how any Christian
can survive, let alone live life
as more than a conqueror,
apart from a quiet time alone with God.
KAY ARTHUR

MORE FROM GOD'S WORD

To every thing there is a season . . .
a time to keep silence, and a time to speak.
ECCLESIASTES 3:1, 7 KJV

Truly my soul silently waits for God;
from Him comes my salvation.
PSALM 62:1 NKJV

Listen in silence before me.
ISAIAH 41:1 NLT

Be still, and know that I am God.
PSALM 46:10 KJV

Now in the morning, having risen
a long while before daylight,
He went out and departed to a solitary place;
and there He prayed.
MARK 1:35 NKJV

A TIMELY TIP

You live in a noisy world filled with distractions, interruptions, and occasional frustrations, a world where silence is in short supply. But God wants you to carve out quiet moments with Him. Silence is, indeed, golden. Value yours.

80

RENEWAL

HE CAN RESTORE YOUR STRENGTH

You are being renewed in the spirit of your minds;
you put on the new self, the one created according
to God's likeness in righteousness and purity of the truth.
EPHESIANS 4:23–24 HCSB

On occasion, the demands of daily life can drain us of our strength and rob us of the joy that is rightfully ours in Christ. When we find ourselves anxious, discouraged, or worse, there is a source from which we can draw the power needed to recharge our spiritual batteries. That source is God.

When we genuinely lift our hearts and prayers to the Lord, He renews our strength.

Are you troubled or anxious? Take your anxieties to God in prayer. Are you weak or worried? Delve deeply into God's holy Word and sense His presence in the quiet moments of the early morning. Are you spiritually exhausted? Call upon fellow believers to support you, and call upon Christ to renew your spirit and your life. The Lord will never let you down. To the contrary, He will always lift you up if you ask Him to. And the best moment to ask for His help is always the present one.

MORE THOUGHTS ABOUT RENEWAL

God is not running an antique shop!
He is making all things new!
VANCE HAVNER

Are you weak? Weary? Confused?
Troubled? Pressured? How is your
relationship with God? Is it held
in its place of priority? I believe the greater
the pressure, the greater your need
for time alone with Him.
KAY ARTHUR

God specializes in giving people a fresh start.
RICK WARREN

The creation of a new heart,
the renewing of a right spirit is an
omnipotent work of God.
Leave it to the Creator.
HENRY DRUMMOND

Our Lord never drew power from Himself;
He drew it always from His Father.
OSWALD CHAMBERS

More from God's Word

*Now the God of all grace, who called you
to His eternal glory in Christ Jesus, will personally restore,
establish, strengthen, and support you.*
1 Peter 5:10 HCSB

*Those who hope in the LORD will renew their strength.
They will soar on wings like eagles; they will run
and not grow weary, they will walk and not be faint.*
Isaiah 40:31 NIV

*Finally, brothers, rejoice. Become mature,
be encouraged, be of the same mind, be at peace,
and the God of love and peace will be with you.*
2 Corinthians 13:11 HCSB

*Remember ye not the former things, neither consider
the things of old. Behold, I will do a new thing.*
Isaiah 43:18–19 KJV

*Therefore, if anyone is in Christ, he is a new creation; old
things have passed away; behold, all things have become new.*
2 Corinthians 5:17 NKJV

A Timely Tip

God can make all things new, including you. When you are anxious or fearful, He can renew your spirit and restore your strength. Your job, of course, is to let Him.

81

SAYING NO

YES, YOU HAVE THE RIGHT TO SAY NO

*Let us lay aside every weight, and the sin
which so easily ensnares us, and let us run
with endurance the race that is set before us.*
HEBREWS 12:1 NKJV

If you haven't yet learned to say no—to say it politely, firmly, and often—you're inviting untold stress into your life. Why? Because if you can't say no (when appropriate), some people will take advantage of your good nature.

If you have trouble standing up for yourself, perhaps you're afraid that you'll be rejected. But here's a tip: don't worry too much about rejection, especially when you're rejected for doing the right thing.

Pleasing other people is a good thing up to a point. But you must never allow your "willingness to please" to interfere with your own good judgment or with God's priorities. God gave you a conscience for a reason: to inform you about the things you need to do as well as the things you don't need to do. It's up to you to follow your conscience wherever it may lead, even if it means making unpopular decisions. Your job, simply put, is to be popular with God, not people.

MORE THOUGHTS ABOUT SAYING NO

Learn to say "no" to the good
so you can say "yes" to the best.
JOHN MAXWELL

Prescription for a happier and healthier life:
resolve to slow your pace; learn to say no gracefully;
reject the temptation to chase after more pleasures,
more hobbies, and more social entanglements.
JAMES DOBSON

Efficiency is enhanced not by
what we accomplish but
more often by what we relinquish.
CHARLES SWINDOLL

As you live your life,
you must localize and define it.
You cannot do everything.
PHILLIPS BROOKS

You must learn to say no when
something is not right for you.
LEONTYNE PRICE

More from God's Word

Discretion will protect you and understanding will guard you.
PROVERBS 2:11 NIV

Keep your eyes focused on what is right,
and look straight ahead to what is good.
PROVERBS 4:25 NCV

The fear of man is a snare, but the one who
trusts in the LORD is protected.
PROVERBS 29:25 HCSB

My son, if sinners entice you, don't be persuaded.
PROVERBS 1:10 HCSB

Obviously, I'm not trying to win the approval of people,
but of God. If pleasing people were my goal,
I would not be Christ's servant.
GALATIANS 1:10 NLT

A Timely Tip

You can't do everything, which means that you need to learn how to say no politely and often. Sometimes people make unreasonable requests, and when they do, you have the right to decline without feeling guilty.

82

SELF-CONFIDENCE

BUILDING SELF-CONFIDENCE

You are my hope; O Lord GOD, You are my confidence.
PSALM 71:5 NASB

Do you believe that you deserve the best, and do you believe that you can achieve the best? Or have you convinced yourself that you're a second-tier talent who'll be lucky to finish far back in the pack? Before you answer these questions, remember this: God sent His Son so that you might enjoy the abundant life that Jesus describes in the familiar words of John 10:10. But God's gifts are not guaranteed—it's up to you to claim them.

If you want to achieve the best that life has to offer, you must put the self-fulfilling prophecy to work for you. How? By convincing yourself beyond a shadow of a doubt that you have the ability to earn the rewards you desire. You must become sold on yourself—sold on your skills, sold on your opportunities, sold on your potential, sold on your attitude, and sold on your character. If you're sold on yourself, chances are the world will soon become sold too. And the results will be beautiful.

MORE THOUGHTS ABOUT SELF-CONFIDENCE

*You need to make the right decision—
firmly and decisively—and then
stick with it, with God's help.*

BILLY GRAHAM

Never yield to gloomy anticipation.

LETTIE COWMAN

*Confidence in the natural world is self-reliance;
in the spiritual world, it is God-reliance.*

OSWALD CHAMBERS

*If you doubt you can accomplish something,
you can't accomplish it. Instead, you have
to be confident in yourself and you need
to be tough enough to follow through.*

ROSALYNN CARTER

*We need to recognize that lack of confidence
does not equal humility. In fact,
genuinely humble people have enormous
confidence because it rests in a great God.*

BETH MOORE

More from God's Word

So we may boldly say: "The LORD is my helper;
I will not fear. What can man do to me?"
HEBREWS 13:6 NKJV

I lift up my eyes to the mountains—where does my help come from?
My help comes from the LORD, the Maker of heaven and earth.
PSALM 121:1-2 NIV

Be strong and courageous, and do the work.
Don't be afraid or discouraged, for the LORD God,
my God, is with you. He won't leave you or forsake you.
1 CHRONICLES 28:20 HCSB

Be on guard. Stand firm in the faith.
Be courageous. Be strong.
1 CORINTHIANS 16:13 NLT

I have come that they may have life,
and that they may have it more abundantly.
JOHN 10:10 NKJV

A Timely Tip

Don't make the mistake of selling yourself short. No matter the size of your challenges, you can be sure that you and God, working together, can handle them. The next time you're tempted to give up on yourself, remember that God will never, never, never give up on you. And with God on your side, you have nothing to fear.

83

SELF-DISCIPLINE

THE POWER OF SELF-DISCIPLINE

*For the Spirit God gave us does not make us timid,
but gives us power, love and self-discipline.*
2 TIMOTHY 1:7 NIV

God's Word reminds us again and again that our Creator expects us to lead disciplined lives. God doesn't reward laziness, misbehavior, or apathy. To the contrary, He expects us to behave with dignity and discipline. But ours is a world in which dignity and discipline are often in short supply.

We live in a world in which leisure is glorified and indifference is often glamorized. But God has other plans. God gives us talents, and He expects us to use them. But it is not always easy to cultivate those talents. Sometimes we must invest countless hours (or, in some cases, many years) honing our skills. And that's perfectly okay with God, because He understands that self-discipline is a blessing, not a burden.

Proverbs 23:12 advises: "Apply your heart to discipline and your ears to words of knowledge" (NASB). And 2 Peter 1:5–6 teaches, "Make every effort to supplement your faith with goodness, goodness with knowledge, knowledge with self-control, self-control with endurance, endurance with godliness" (HSCB). Thus, God's Word is clear: we must exercise self-discipline in all matters.

When we pause to consider how much work needs to be done, we realize that self-discipline is not simply a proven way to get ahead, it's also an integral part of God's plan for our lives. If we genuinely seek to be faithful stewards of our time, our talents, and our resources, we must adopt a disciplined approach to life. Otherwise, our talents are wasted and our resources are squandered.

Life's greatest rewards seldom fall into our laps; to the contrary, our greatest accomplishments usually require work, perseverance, and discipline. May we, as disciplined believers, be willing to work for the rewards we so earnestly desire.

MORE THOUGHTS ABOUT SELF-DISCIPLINE

Action springs not from thought,
but from a readiness for responsibility.
DIETRICH BONHOEFFER

Pray as though everything depended on God.
Work as though everything depended on you.
ST. AUGUSTINE

There's some task which the God of all the universe,
the great Creator has for you to do, and which will
remain undone and incomplete, until by faith
and obedience, you step into the will of God.
ALAN REDPATH

Each day you must say to yourself, "Today I am going to begin."
JEAN PIERRE DE CAUSSADE

MORE FROM GOD'S WORD

Well done, good and faithful servant; you were faithful over a few things, I will make you ruler over many things. Enter into the joy of your lord.
MATTHEW 25:21 NKJV

For the kingdom of God is not a matter of talk but of power.
1 CORINTHIANS 4:20 HCSB

When you make a vow to God, do not delay to fulfill it. He has no pleasure in fools; fulfill your vow.
ECCLESIASTES 5:4 NIV

Whenever we have the opportunity, we should do good to everyone—especially to those in the family of faith.
GALATIANS 6:10 NLT

But prove yourselves doers of the word, and not merely hearers who delude themselves.
JAMES 1:22 NASB

A TIMELY TIP

If you're planning on becoming a disciplined person "someday" in the distant future, you're deluding yourself. The best day to begin exercising self-discipline is this one.

84

SELF-EXAMINATION

GETTING TO KNOW YOURSELF

*Why worry about a speck in your friend's eye when you
have a log in your own? How can you think of saying to your
friend, "Let me help you get rid of that speck in your eye,"
when you can't see past the log in your own eye? Hypocrite!
First get rid of the log in your own eye; then you will see
well enough to deal with the speck in your friend's eye.*
MATTHEW 7:3–5 NLT

If you're looking for better ways to manage your emotions, it's tempting to focus exclusively on the stressors around you. But it's also helpful to look at the stressors within you. Perhaps you're over-estimating the size of your problems; perhaps you're being overly pessimistic; maybe you're being too hard on other people. Or perhaps you have other issues that are stealing your joy day by day and moment by moment.

If you're experiencing hurtful feelings that just won't go away, it's time to schedule an appointment with your pastor, or with a pastoral counselor, or with a mental health professional. These people can help you look inside to discover, and then banish, the hurtful feelings or exaggerated thought patterns that may be holding you back. When you examine yourself—as you look at your own personal history and your habitual ways of dealing with the world around you—you may decide it's time to make some changes. If so, here's twofold advice: get started now and be patient.

Being patient with other people can be difficult. But sometimes we find it even more difficult to be patient with ourselves. We have high expectations and lofty goals. We want to accomplish things now, not later. And, of course, we want our lives to unfold according to our own timetables, not God's.

Throughout the Bible, we are instructed that patience is the companion of wisdom. God's message, then, is clear: we must be patient with all people, beginning with that particular person who stares back at us each time we gaze into the mirror. So if you happen to be your own worst critic—or if you expect perfection from yourself (not to mention others)—it's time to reconsider. When you look inward—and upward—you'll discover that life doesn't have to be perfect to be wonderful.

MORE THOUGHTS ABOUT SELF-EXAMINATION

The man who does not like self-examination may be pretty certain that things need examining.
C. H. SPURGEON

A humble knowledge of oneself is a surer road to God than a deep searching of the sciences.
THOMAS Á KEMPIS

The man who has no inner life is the slave to his surroundings.
HENRI FRÉDÉRIC AMIEL

MORE FROM GOD'S WORD

You shall know the truth, and the truth shall make you free.
JOHN 8:32 NKJV

Commit yourself to instruction;
listen carefully to words of knowledge.
PROVERBS 23:12 NLT

I urge you to live a life worthy of the calling you have received.
EPHESIANS 4:1 NIV

Let the wise listen and add to their learning,
and let the discerning get guidance.
PROVERBS 1:5 NIV

A TIMELY TIP

As you journey through life, you should continue to become better aquatinted with yourself. How? One way is to examine the patterns in your own life, and understand that unless you make the conscious effort to change those patterns, you're likely to repeat them. So if you don't like some of the results you've earned, change your behaviors. The sooner you change, the sooner your results will change too.

85

SHAME

BEYOND SHAME

Let us come near to God with a sincere heart and a sure faith,
because we have been made free from a guilty conscience,
and our bodies have been washed with pure water.
HEBREWS 10:22 NCV

Have you done things you're ashamed of? If so, welcome to a very large club. Even the very best people on the planet have done things that only God can forgive. But the good news is this: whenever we admit our shortcomings to God and ask for His forgiveness, He gives it.

There's nothing any of us can do to redeem ourselves from sin; that's something only God can do. So what can we do? We can allow God's Son into our hearts and allow Him to do what we cannot.

Shame is a form of spiritual cancer; it can be deadly, but it is treatable. The treatment begins when we acknowledge our sins and ask for God's mercy. But it doesn't end there. Once God forgives us, we still have work to do: we must forgive ourselves.

God knows all your imperfections, all your faults, and all your shortcomings . . . and He loves you anyway. And because God loves you, you can—and should—feel good about the person you see when you look into the mirror. God's love is bigger and more powerful than anybody (including you) can imagine, but His love is very real. So do yourself a favor right now: accept God's love with open arms. And while you're at it, remember this: even when you don't love yourself very much, God loves you. And God is always right.

MORE THOUGHTS ABOUT GUILT AND SHAME

The purpose of guilt is to bring us to Jesus.
Once we are there, then its purpose is finished.
If we continue to make ourselves guilty—
to blame ourselves—then that is a sin in itself.
CORRIE TEN BOOM

The most marvelous ingredient in
the forgiveness of God is that He
also forgets, the one thing a human being
cannot do. With God, forgetting is a
divine attribute. God's forgiveness forgets.
OSWALD CHAMBERS

If God forgives us and we do not
forgive ourselves, we make
ourselves greater than God.
EDWIN LOUIS COLE

God does not wish us to remember
what He is willing to forget.
GEORGE A. BUTTRICK

MORE FROM GOD'S WORD

Be gracious to me, God, according to Your faithful love;
according to Your abundant compassion, blot out my rebellion.
Wash away my guilt, and cleanse me from my sin.
PSALM 51:1–2 HCSB

If we confess our sins, He is faithful and righteous to forgive
us our sins and to cleanse us from all unrighteousness.
1 JOHN 1:9 NASB

Create in me a pure heart, God,
and make my spirit right again.
PSALM 51:10 NCV

How can I know all the sins lurking in my heart?
Cleanse me from these hidden faults. Keep your servant
from deliberate sins! Don't let them control me.
Then I will be free of guilt and innocent of great sin.
PSALM 19:12–13 NLT

Guard your heart above all else, for it is the source of life.
PROVERBS 4:23 HCSB

A TIMELY TIP

If you're being victimized by shame, it's time to have a heart-to-heart talk with your Creator. If you've asked for God's forgiveness, He has given it. And because He has forgiven you, you should be quick to forgive yourself and make peace with your past. To do otherwise is to hold yourself to a different standard than God does.

86

SIMPLICITY

A simple life in the Fear-of-God is better
than a rich life with a ton of headaches.
PROVERBS 15:16 MSG

Want to reduce stress? Here's a simple solution: simplify your life. Unfortunately, simplification is easier said than done. After all, you live in a world where simplicity is in short supply.

Think for a moment about the complexity of your everyday life and compare it to the lives of your ancestors. Certainly you are the beneficiary of many technological innovations, but those innovations have come at a price: in all likelihood, your world is highly complex. Unless you take firm control of your time and your life, you may be overwhelmed by an anxiety-producing, stress-inducing tidal wave of obligations that leave you spiritually and emotionally drained.

Time and again God's Word warns us against the trap of materialism. And as Proverbs 15:16 reminds us, a simple life with God is vastly superior to its materialistic alternative. So do yourself and your loved ones a favor: keep your life as simple as possible. Simplicity is, indeed, genius. By simplifying your life, you are destined to improve it.

More Thoughts about Simplicity

The more complicated life becomes,
the more we need to quiet our souls before God.
ELISABETH ELLIOT

The simplicity which is in Christ
is rarely found among us. In its stead
are programs, methods, organizations,
and a world of nervous activities
which occupy time and attention.
A. W. TOZER

Simplifying your life means focusing
on who you are physically, emotionally,
and spiritually. If you want to
choose joy daily, that's the place to start.
KAY WARREN

Happy is the person who has
learned to rejoice in the simple
and beautiful things around him.
BILLY GRAHAM

The characteristic of the life
of a saint is essentially elemental simplicity.
OSWALD CHAMBERS

More from God's Word

Whoever becomes simple and elemental again,
like this child, will rank high in God's kingdom.
MATTHEW 18:4 MSG

The LORD preserves the simple;
I was brought low, and He saved me.
PSALM 116:6 NASB

Seek to lead a quiet life,
to mind your own business,
and to work with your own hands,
as we commanded you.
1 THESSALONIANS 4:11 HCSB

God has called us to peace.
1 CORINTHIANS 7:15 NKJV

May mercy, peace,
and love be multiplied to you.
JUDE 1:2 HCSB

A Timely Tip

Perhaps you think that the more things you acquire, the happier you'll be. If so, think again. Simplicity and peace are two concepts that are closely related. Complexity and peace are not. When in doubt, take the simpler route.

87

SLEEP

ARE YOU GETTING ENOUGH REST?

The LORD shall give thee rest
from thy sorrow, and from thy fear.
ISAIAH 14:3 KJV

You inhabit an interconnected world that never slows down and never shuts off. The world tempts you to stay up late watching the news or surfing the Internet or checking out social media or gaming or doing countless other activities that gobble up your time and distract you from more important tasks. But too much late-night screen time robs you of something you need very badly: sleep.

Are you going to bed at a reasonable hour and sleeping through the night? If so, you're both wise and blessed. But if you're staying up late with your eyes glued to a screen, you may be increasing your anxiety level, and you're most certainly putting your long-term health at risk. To make matters worse, you may be wasting lots of time too.

So the next time you're tempted to engage in late-night, time-gobbling activities, resist the temptation. Instead, turn your thoughts and prayers to God. And when you're finished, turn off the lights and go to bed. You need rest more than you need entertainment.

More Thoughts about Rest

Take rest. A field that has
rested gives a beautiful crop.
OVID

Think in the morning.
Act in the noon. Eat in the evening.
Sleep in the night.
WILLIAM BLAKE

It is a common experience that
a problem difficult at night is resolved
in the morning after the committee
of sleep has worked on it.
JOHN STEINBECK

Early to bed and early to rise,
makes a man healthy, wealthy, and wise.
BEN FRANKLIN

Go to bed. Whatever you're
staying up for isn't worth it.
ANDY ROONEY

More from God's Word

Take My yoke upon you and learn from Me, because
I am gentle and humble in heart, and you will find rest
for your souls. For My yoke is easy and My burden is light.
MATTHEW 11:29–30 HCSB

In quietness and in confidence shall be your strength.
ISAIAH 30:15 KJV

Return unto thy rest, O my soul;
for the LORD hath dealt bountifully with thee.
PSALM 116:7 KJV

Come unto me, all ye that labor
and are heavy laden, and I will give you rest.
MATTHEW 11:28 KJV

Finally, brothers, rejoice. Become mature,
be encouraged, be of the same mind, be at peace,
and the God of love and peace will be with you.
2 CORINTHIANS 13:11 HCSB

A Timely Tip

If you're chronically anxious, fearful, or tired, perhaps you need a little more shuteye. Try this experiment: turn off all your devices and go to bed at a reasonable hour. You'll be amazed at how good you feel when you get eight hours' sleep.

88

SPIRITUAL GROWTH

SEIZE EVERY OPPORTUNITY FOR SPIRITUAL GROWTH

*I remind you to fan into flames
the spiritual gift God gave you.*
2 TIMOTHY 1:6 NLT

The path to spiritual maturity unfolds day by day, through good times and hard times. Each day offers the opportunity to worship God and to be blessed by the richness of our relationship with Him.

In those quiet moments when we open our hearts to the Father, the One who made us keeps remaking us. He gives us direction, hope, perspective, and courage. And the appropriate moment to accept those spiritual gifts is always the present one.

Are you feeling anxious? Are you fearful? Are you enduring tough times that have left your head spinning? If so, you can be certain that God still has important lessons to teach you. So ask yourself this: What lesson is God trying to teach me today? And then go about the business of learning it.

MORE THOUGHTS ABOUT SPIRITUAL GROWTH

God's ultimate goal for your life
on earth is not comfort,
but character development.
He wants you to grow up spiritually
and become like Christ.

RICK WARREN

God will help us become the people
we are meant to be, if only we will ask Him.

HANNAH WHITALL SMITH

Mark it down. You will never
go where God is not.

MAX LUCADO

Grow, dear friends, but grow,
I beseech you, in God's way,
which is the only true way.

HANNAH WHITALL SMITH

The vigor of our spiritual life
will be in exact proportion to the place
held by the Bible in our life and thoughts.

GEORGE MUELLER

More from God's Word

Grow in the grace and knowledge of our Lord and Savior Jesus Christ. To Him be the glory both now and forever. Amen.
2 PETER 3:18 NKJV

But endurance must do its complete work, so that you may be mature and complete, lacking nothing.
JAMES 1:4 HCSB

Leave inexperience behind, and you will live; pursue the way of understanding.
PROVERBS 9:6 HCSB

Be not conformed to this world: but be ye transformed by the renewing of your mind, that ye may prove what is that good, and acceptable, and perfect will of God.
ROMANS 12:2 KJV

So let us stop going over the basic teachings about Christ again and again. Let us go on instead and become mature in our understanding.
HEBREWS 6:1 NLT

A Timely Tip

When it comes to your faith, God doesn't want you to stand still. He wants you to keep growing. And sometimes He places people along your path who, because of their personalities, can teach you lessons you could have learned in no other way. The Lord knows that spiritual maturity is a lifelong journey. You should know it too.

89

STARTING OVER

IF YOU'RE STARTING OVER

Then the One seated on the throne said,
"Look! I am making everything new."
REVELATION 21:5 HCSB

If you're experiencing tough times—or if you're starting over from scratch—you may feel like you're entering an entirely new phase of life. If so, congratulations. Your fresh start is an occasion to be celebrated. God has a perfect plan for your life, and He has the power to make all things new.

As you think about your future—and as you consider the countless opportunities that will be woven into the fabric of the days ahead—be sure to include God in your plans. When you do, He will guide your steps and light your path.

Perhaps you want to change the direction of your life, or perhaps you're determined to make major modifications in the way you live or the way you think. If so, you and God, working together, can do it. But don't expect change to be easy or instant. God expects you to do your fair share of the work, and that's as it should be.

If you're going through a spiritual growth spurt, don't be surprised if you experience a few spiritual growing pains. Why?

Because real transformation begins on the inside and works its way out from there. And sometimes the "working out" is painful. Lasting change doesn't occur "out there"; it occurs "in here." It occurs, not in the shifting sands of your own particular circumstances, but in the quiet depths of your own obedient heart. So if you're in search of a new beginning or, for that matter, a new you, don't expect changing circumstances to miraculously transform you into the person you want to become. Transformation starts with God, and it starts in the silent center of a humble human heart—like yours.

MORE THOUGHTS ABOUT NEW BEGINNINGS

What saves a man is to take a step. Then another step.
C. S. LEWIS

The best preparation for the future is the present well seen to, and the last duty done.
GEORGE MACDONALD

Whoever you are, wherever you are, whatever you've been through, it's never too late to begin again.
JOYCE MEYER

Are you in earnest? Seize this very minute. What you can do, or dream you can, begin it. Boldness has genius, power, and magic in it.
JOHANN WOLFGANG VON GOETHE

MORE FROM GOD'S WORD

"For I know the plans I have for you"—this is the LORD's declaration—"plans for your welfare, not for disaster, to give you a future and a hope."
JEREMIAH 29:11 HCSB

Your old sinful self has died, and your new life is kept with Christ in God.
COLOSSIANS 3:3 NCV

There is one thing I always do. Forgetting the past and straining toward what is ahead, I keep trying to reach the goal and get the prize for which God called me.
PHILIPPIANS 3:13–14 NCV

You are being renewed in the spirit of your minds; you put on the new self, the one created according to God's likeness in righteousness and purity of the truth.
EPHESIANS 4:23–24 HCSB

Do not remember the former things, nor consider the things of old. Behold, I will do a new thing.
ISAIAH 43:18–19 NKJV

A TIMELY TIP

If you're graduating into a new phase of life, be sure to make God your partner. When you do, He'll guide your steps; He'll help carry your burdens; and He'll help you focus on the opportunities of the future, not the losses of the past.

90

STRENGTH

FINDING STRENGTH TO MANAGE YOUR EMOTIONS

He gives strength to the weary,
and to him who lacks might He increases power.

ISAIAH 40:29 NASB

God's love and support never change. From the cradle to the grave, God has promised to give you the strength to meet any challenge. God has promised to lift you up and guide your steps if you let Him. God has promised that when you entrust your life to Him completely and without reservation, He will give you the courage to face any trial and the wisdom to live in His righteousness.

Are you an energized Christian? You should be. But if you're not, you must seek emotional strength from the source that will never fail: that source, of course, is your heavenly Father. And rest assured—when you sincerely petition Him, He will give you all the strength you need to live victoriously for Him.

God has promised to protect us, and He intends to keep His promise. In a world filled with dangers and temptations, God is the ultimate armor. In a world filled with misleading messages, God's Word is the ultimate truth. In a world filled with more frustrations than we can count, God's Son offers the ultimate peace.

More Thoughts about God's Strength

God is in control. He may not take away trials or make detours for us, but He strengthens us through them.
BILLY GRAHAM

Faith is a strong power, mastering any difficulty in the strength of the Lord who made heaven and earth.
CORRIE TEN BOOM

The truth is, God's strength is fully revealed when our strength is depleted.
LIZ CURTIS HIGGS

The strength that we claim from God's Word does not depend on circumstances. Circumstances will be difficult, but our strength will be sufficient.
CORRIE TEN BOOM

God will give us the strength and resources we need to live through any situation in life that He ordains.
BILLY GRAHAM

Nothing on earth compares to the strength God is willing to interject into lives caught in the act of believing.
BETH MOORE

More from God's Word

I can do all things through Christ who strengthens me.
PHILIPPIANS 4:13 NKJV

My grace is sufficient for you,
for my power is made perfect in weakness.
2 CORINTHIANS 12:9 NIV

Be strong and courageous, and do the work.
Don't be afraid or discouraged, for the LORD God,
my God, is with you. He won't leave you or forsake you.
1 CHRONICLES 28:20 HCSB

Have faith in the LORD your God,
and you will stand strong.
Have faith in his prophets, and you will succeed.
2 CHRONICLES 20:20 NCV

The LORD is my strength and my song;
He has become my salvation.
EXODUS 15:2 HCSB

A Timely Tip

Need strength? Slow down, get more rest, engage in regular, sensible exercise, and turn your troubles over to God . . . but not necessarily in that order.

91

STRESS

MANAGING STRESS

Come unto me, all ye that labor
and are heavy laden, and I will give you rest.
MATTHEW 11:28 KJV

Stressful days are an inevitable fact of modern life. And how do we best cope with the challenges of our demanding twenty-first-century world? By turning our days and our lives over to God. Elisabeth Elliot writes, "If my life is surrendered to God, all is well. Let me not grab it back, as though it were in peril in His hand but would be safer in mine!" Yet even the most devout Christian may, at times, seek to grab the reins and proclaim, "I'm in charge!" To do so is foolish, prideful, and stress-inducing.

When we seek to impose our own wills upon the world—or upon other people—we invite stress into our lives . . . needlessly. But when we turn our lives and our hearts over to God—when we accept His will instead of seeking vainly to impose our own—we discover the inner peace that can be ours through Him.

Do you feel overwhelmed by the stresses of daily life? Turn your concerns and your prayers over to God. Trust Him. Trust Him completely. Trust Him today. Trust Him always. Whatever your concerns, whatever your challenges, hand them over to God completely and without reservation. He knows your needs and will meet those needs in His own way and in His own time if you let Him. He's always with you, always in your corner, always ready to help. And the rest, of course, is up to you.

MORE THOUGHTS ABOUT MANAGING STRESS

*Beware of having so much to do
that you really do nothing at all because
you do not wait upon God to do it aright.*
C. H. SPURGEON

*There are many burned-out people
who think more is always better,
who deem it unspiritual to say no.*
SARAH YOUNG

God specializes in giving people a fresh start.
RICK WARREN

Life is strenuous. See that your clock does not run down.
LETTIE COWMAN

*The more comfortable we are
with mystery in our journey,
the more rest we will know along the way.*
JOHN ELDREDGE

MORE FROM GOD'S WORD

Live peaceful and quiet lives
in all godliness and holiness.
1 TIMOTHY 2:2 NIV

I find rest in God; only he gives me hope.
PSALM 62:5 NCV

You, LORD, give true peace to those
who depend on you, because they trust you.
ISAIAH 26:3 NCV

Peace I leave with you; My peace I give to you;
not as the world gives do I give to you.
Do not let your heart be troubled, nor let it be fearful.
JOHN 14:27 NASB

And the peace of God, which transcends
all understanding, will guard your hearts
and your minds in Christ Jesus.
PHILIPPIANS 4:7 NIV

A TIMELY TIP

If you're serious about beating stress, reducing anxiety, and overcoming fear, you must form the habit of talking to God first thing every morning. He's available. Are you?

92

SUFFERING

WHEN YOU'RE SUFFERING

The God of all grace, who called you to his eternal glory
in Christ, after you have suffered a little while, will himself
restore you and make you strong, firm and steadfast.
1 PETER 5:10 NIV

All of us face times of hardship and emotional strain. When we face the inevitable difficulties of life here on earth, we can seek help from family, from friends, and from God . . . but not necessarily in that order.

Barbara Johnson writes, "There is no way around suffering. We have to go through it to get to the other side." And the best way "to get to the other side" of suffering is to get there with God. When we turn open hearts to Him in heartfelt prayer, He will answer—in His own time and according to His own plan—and He will heal us.

And while we are waiting for God's plans to unfold and for His healing touch to restore us, we can be comforted in the knowledge that our Creator can overcome any obstacle, even if we cannot. The Psalmist writes, "Weeping may endure for a night, but joy comes in the morning" (Psalm 30:5 NKJV). But when we are hurting, the morning may seem very far away. It is not. God promises that He is "near to those who have a broken heart" (Psalm 34:18 NKJV).

If you are experiencing the intense pain of a recent loss, or if you are still mourning a loss from long ago, perhaps you are now ready to begin the next stage of your journey with God. If so, be mindful of this fact: the loving heart of God is sufficient to meet any challenge, including yours.

MORE THOUGHTS ABOUT SUFFERING

God is sufficient for all our needs, for every problem, for every difficulty, for every broken heart, for every human sorrow.
PETER MARSHALL

The promises of God's Word sustain us in our suffering, and we know Jesus sympathizes and empathizes with us in our darkest hour.
BILL BRIGHT

You don't have to be alone in your hurt! Comfort is yours. Joy is an option. And it's all been made possible by your Savior.
JONI EARECKSON TADA

Suffering is never for nothing. It is that you and I might be conformed to the image of Christ.
ELISABETH ELLIOT

God whispers to us in our pleasures, speaks in our conscience, but shouts in our pains: it is His megaphone to rouse a deaf world.
C. S. LEWIS

More from God's Word

In my distress I called upon the LORD,
and cried unto my God: he heard my voice.
PSALM 18:6 KJV

I have heard your prayer; I have seen your tears.
Look, I will heal you.
2 KINGS 20:5 HCSB

I have told you these things so that in Me
you may have peace. You will have suffering in this world.
Be courageous! I have conquered the world.
JOHN 16:33 HCSB

You who are now hungry are blessed, because you will be filled.
You who now weep are blessed, because you will laugh.
LUKE 6:21 HCSB

Is anyone among you suffering? He should pray.
JAMES 5:13 HCSB

A Timely Tip

All of us must, from time to time, endure unfortunate circumstances that test our faith. No man or woman, no matter how righteous, is exempt. Christians, however, face their suffering and grief with the ultimate armor: God's promises. God will help heal us if we welcome Him into our hearts.

93

TAKING ACTION

YOU'RE NOT STUCK

Therefore, with your minds ready for action,
be serious and set your hope completely on
the grace to be brought to you at the revelation of Jesus Christ.
1 PETER 1:13 HCSB

Are you in the habit of doing what needs to be done when it needs to be done, or are you more likely to put off the harder tasks until some vaguely defined date in the future? If you've acquired the habit of doing your most important work first (even if you'd rather be doing something else), congratulations! You're not only doing the right thing; you're also reducing anxiety and stress. But if you find yourself putting off all those unpleasant tasks until later (or never), it's time to think about the consequences of your behavior.

Chronic procrastinators unintentionally squeeze the joy out of their own lives and the lives of their loved ones. So your job is to summon the determination, the courage, and the wisdom to defeat Old Man Procrastination whenever he arrives at your doorstep.

You can free yourself from the emotional quicksand by paying less attention to your fears and more attention to your responsibilities. So when you're faced with a difficult choice or an unpleasant responsibility, don't spend endless hours fretting over your fate. Simply seek God's counsel and get busy. And while you're at it, remember that you're not stuck *unless* you allow yourself to be stuck.

MORE THOUGHTS ABOUT DOING IT NOW

The fear of attempting something big immobilizes people. To begin a task is usually the toughest step.
JOHN MAXWELL

Action springs not from thought, but from a readiness for responsibility.
DIETRICH BONHOEFFER

The one word in the spiritual vocabulary is now.
OSWALD CHAMBERS

There's some task which the God of all the universe, the great Creator, has for you to do, and which will remain undone and incomplete, until by faith and obedience, you step into the will of God.
ALAN REDPATH

Authentic faith cannot help but act.
BETH MOORE

Pray as though everything depended on God. Work as though everything depended on you.
ST. AUGUSTINE

MORE FROM GOD'S WORD

But prove yourselves doers of the word,
and not merely hearers who delude themselves.
JAMES 1:22 NASB

When you make a vow to God, do not delay to fulfill it.
He has no pleasure in fools; fulfill your vow.
ECCLESIASTES 5:4 NIV

For the kingdom of God is not a matter of talk but of power.
1 CORINTHIANS 4:20 HCSB

Whenever we have the opportunity, we should do good
to everyone—especially to those in the family of faith.
GALATIANS 6:10 NLT

Well done, good and faithful servant; you were faithful
over a few things, I will make you ruler over many things.
Enter into the joy of your lord.
MATTHEW 25:21 NKJV

A TIMELY TIP

If you've been putting off dealing with an emotionally charged
situation or a difficult person, pray for God's wisdom and His
strength. Ask Him to help you deal with the problem in the best
way possible, which usually means responding sooner rather than
later.

94

TAKING RESPONSIBILITY

YOU'RE RESPONSIBLE

But each person should examine his own work,
and then he will have a reason for boasting in himself alone,
and not in respect to someone else.
For each person will have to carry his own load.

GALATIANS 6:4–5 HCSB

It's time to state a rather obvious fact: you're responsible for your own behavior and other people are responsible for theirs. But if you're not careful, you may find yourself spending too much time worrying about the myriad ways that other people are misbehaving and not enough time focusing on your own responsibilities. So instead of trying to improve other people, a better strategy is simply this: get busy trying to improve yourself.

God's Word encourages us to take responsibility for our actions, but the world tempts us to do otherwise. The media tries to convince us that we're "victims" of our upbringing, our government, our economic strata, or our circumstances, thus ignoring the countless blessings—and the gift of free will—that God has given each of us. We're also tempted to blame our problems on the people who make our lives difficult. It's an easy excuse, but a shortsighted one.

Your heavenly Father wants you to be a faithful steward of the gifts He has given you. But you live in a society that may encourage you to do otherwise. You face countless temptations to squander your time, your resources, and your talents. So you must be keenly aware of the inevitable distractions that can waste your time, your energy, and your opportunities.

God has blessed you with unique opportunities to serve Him, and He has given you every tool that you need to do so. Today, accept this challenge: value the talent that God has given you, nourish it, make it grow, and share it with the world. After all, the best way to say "thank You" for God's gifts is to use them.

So who's responsible for your behavior? And who's responsible for utilizing the talents that the Lord has given you? God's Word says that you are. It's your life, which means that the person you see in the mirror is the very same person who's responsible for the things you do, the things you say, and the way you utilize your talents. No exceptions.

MORE THOUGHTS ABOUT TAKING RESPONSIBILITY

*Man must cease attributing his problems
to his environment, and learn again to exercise his will—
his personal responsibility in the realm of faith and morals.*
ALBERT SCHWEITZER

*Action springs not from thought,
but from a readiness for responsibility.*
DIETRICH BONHOEFFER

Faithfulness in carrying out present duties
is the best preparation for the future.
FRANÇOIS FÈNELON

MORE FROM GOD'S WORD

So then, each of us will give an account of himself to God.
ROMANS 14:12 HCSB

Better to be patient than powerful;
better to have self-control than to conquer a city.
PROVERBS 16:32 NLT

Then He said to His disciples, "The harvest
is abundant, but the workers are few."
MATTHEW 9:37 HCSB

We must do the works of Him who sent Me while it is day.
Night is coming when no one can work.
JOHN 9:4 HCSB

A TIMELY TIP

It's easy to hold other people accountable, but real accountability begins with the person you see when you look in the mirror. So don't look for someone you can blame; look for something constructive you can do. When you accept responsibility and take the necessary steps to resolve your problems, you'll feel better about yourself *and* you'll get more done. Lots more.

95

THOUGHTS

GUARD YOUR THOUGHTS

Finally, brothers and sisters, whatever is true, whatever is noble,
whatever is right, whatever is pure, whatever is lovely,
whatever is admirable—if anything is
excellent or praiseworthy—think about such things.
PHILIPPIANS 4:8 NIV

How will you direct your thoughts today? Will you obey the words of Philippians 4:8 by dwelling upon those things that are noble, pure, and admirable? Or will you allow your thoughts to be hijacked by the general negativity that seems to dominate our troubled world?

Are you feeling fearful, angry, frustrated, or anxious? Are you so preoccupied with the concerns of this day that you fail to thank God for the promise of eternity? Are you confused, bitter, or pessimistic? If so, God wants to have a little talk with you.

God intends that you be an ambassador for Him, an enthusiastic, hope-filled Christian. But God won't force you to adopt a positive attitude. It's up to you to think positively about your blessings and your opportunities. When you do so, your positive thoughts will generate positive emotions.

So today and every day hereafter, celebrate this life that God has given you by focusing your thoughts and your energies upon things that are excellent and praiseworthy. It's the best way to think and the best way to live.

MORE THOUGHTS ABOUT GUARDING YOUR THOUGHTS

It is the thoughts and intents of the heart that shape a person's life.
JOHN ELDREDGE

Change always starts in your mind.
The way you think determines the way you feel,
and the way you feel influences the way you act.
RICK WARREN

When you think on the powerful truths of Scripture,
God uses His Word to change your way of thinking.
ELIZABETH GEORGE

The things we think are the things that feed our souls.
If we think on pure and lovely things, we shall grow pure
and lovely like them; and the converse is equally true.
HANNAH WHITALL SMITH

Your life today is a result of your thinking yesterday. Your life
tomorrow will be determined by what you think today.
JOHN MAXWELL

More from God's Word

For to be carnally minded is death,
but to be spiritually minded is life and peace.
ROMANS 8:6 NKJV

The peace of God, which surpasses all understanding,
will guard your hearts and minds through Christ Jesus.
PHILIPPIANS 4:7 NKJV

And do not be conformed to this world,
but be transformed by the renewing
of your mind, so that you may prove
what the will of God is, that which
is good and acceptable and perfect.
ROMANS 12:2 NASB

Guard your heart above all else, for it is the source of life.
PROVERBS 4:23 HCSB

Set your mind on things above, not on things on the earth.
COLOSSIANS 3:2 NKJV

A Timely Tip

Negative thoughts have a way of hijacking your emotions. So if you sense that your emotions are beginning to spin out of control, slow down, take a few deep breaths, and try to reconnect with reality. Here are the facts: God's love is real; His peace is real; His support is real. Don't ever let your emotions obscure these truths.

96

TODAY IS A GIFT

REMEMBER THAT
EVERY DAY IS PRECIOUS

*So teach us to number our days,
that we may present to You a heart of wisdom.*
PSALM 90:12 NASB

This day is a blessed gift from God. And as Christians, we have countless reasons to rejoice. Yet on some days, when we experience unwelcome emotions—or when the demands of daily life threaten to overwhelm us—we don't feel much like rejoicing. Instead of celebrating God's glorious creation, we may find ourselves discouraged by the frustrations of today and worried about the uncertainties of tomorrow.

C. H. Spurgeon, the renowned nineteenth-century English clergymen, advised, "Rejoicing is clearly a spiritual command. To ignore it, I need to remind you, is disobedience." As Christians, we are called by our Creator to live abundantly, prayerfully, and joyfully. To do otherwise is to squander His spiritual gifts.

If you're a thoughtful Christian, you're a thankful Christian. Because of your faith, you can face the inevitable challenges and disappointments of each day armed with the joy of Christ and the promise of eternal life. So whatever this day holds for you, begin it and end it with God as your partner and Christ as your Savior. Treasure the time that the Lord has given you. And search for the hidden possibilities that He has placed along your path. This day is a priceless gift from your Creator; use it joyfully and productively. After all, night is coming when no one can work . . .

MORE THOUGHTS ABOUT THE PRECIOUSNESS OF TODAY

Today is mine. Tomorrow is none of my business. If I peer anxiously into the fog of the future, I will strain my spiritual eyes so that I will not see clearly what is required of me now.
ELISABETH ELLIOT

Yesterday is the tomb of time, and tomorrow is the womb of time. Only now is yours.
R. G. LEE

Each day is God's gift of a fresh unspoiled opportunity to live according to His priorities.
ELIZABETH GEORGE

Faith does not concern itself with the entire journey. One step is enough.
LETTIE COWMAN

The one word in the spiritual vocabulary is now.
OSWALD CHAMBERS

MORE FROM GOD'S WORD

This is the day the LORD has made;
let us rejoice and be glad in it.
PSALM 118:24 HCSB

Rejoice always, pray without ceasing,
in everything give thanks;
for this is the will of God in Christ Jesus for you.
1 THESSALONIANS 5:16–18 NKJV

So don't worry about tomorrow,
because tomorrow will have its own worries.
Each day has enough trouble of its own.
MATTHEW 6:34 NCV

Shout to the LORD, all the earth;
be jubilant, shout for joy, and sing.
PSALM 98:4 HCSB

These things I have spoken to you,
that My joy may remain in you,
and that your joy may be full.
JOHN 15:11 NKJV

A TIMELY TIP

Today is a wonderful, one-of-a-kind gift from God. Treat it that way. And as the day unfolds, don't let the minor inconveniences of everyday life rob you of the joy that can—and should—be yours.

97

TRUSTING GOD

Indeed, God is my salvation.
I will trust Him and not be afraid.
ISAIAH 12:2 HCSB

God's instructions to mankind are contained in a book like no other: the Holy Bible. When we obey God's commandments and listen carefully to the conscience He has placed in our hearts, we are secure. But if we disobey our Creator, if we choose to ignore the teachings and the warnings of His Word, we do so at great peril.

If we believe in God, we should also trust in God. Yet sometimes, when we are besieged by fears and doubts, trusting God is hard indeed. Trusting God means entrusting Him with every aspect of our lives as we follow His commandments and pray for His guidance. When we experience the inevitable pains of life here on earth, we must accept His will and seek His healing touch. And at times we must be willing to wait patiently for the Lord to reveal plans that only He can see.

The next time you find your courage tested to the limit, lean upon God's promises. Trust His Son. Remember that God is always near and that He is your protector and your deliverer. When you are worried, anxious, or afraid, call upon Him. God can handle your troubles infinitely better than you can, so turn them over to Him.

Remember that the Lord rules both mountaintops and valleys with limitless wisdom and love, now and forever.

MORE THOUGHTS ABOUT TRUSTING GOD

What you trust to Him you must not worry over nor feel anxious about. Trust and worry cannot go together.
HANNAH WHITALL SMITH

Trust God's Word and His power more than you trust your own feelings and experiences. Remember, your Rock is Christ, and it is the sea that ebbs and flows with the tides, not Him.
LETTIE COWMAN

Never be afraid to trust an unknown future to a known God.
CORRIE TEN BOOM

Once God leads you to make a decision, don't draw back. Instead, trust His leading and believe He goes before you—because He does.
BILLY GRAHAM

Never imagine that you can be a loser by trusting in God.
C. H. SPURGEON

Remember always that there are two things which are more utterly incompatible even than oil and water, and these two are trust and worry.
HANNAH WHITALL SMITH

MORE FROM GOD'S WORD

Jesus said, "Don't let your hearts be troubled.
Trust in God, and trust in me."
JOHN 14:1 NCV

The LORD is my rock, my fortress, and my deliverer,
my God, my mountain where I seek refuge. My shield, the horn
of my salvation, my stronghold, my refuge, and my Savior.
2 SAMUEL 22:2–3 HCSB

Trust in the LORD with all your heart, and lean not
on your own understanding; in all your ways
acknowledge Him, and He shall direct your paths.
PROVERBS 3:5–6 NKJV

The fear of man is a snare, but the one who
trusts in the LORD is protected.
PROVERBS 29:25 HCSB

Those who trust in the LORD are like Mount Zion.
It cannot be shaken; it remains forever.
PSALM 125:1 HCSB

A TIMELY TIP

You can always trust God because He always keeps His promises. The Lord has a plan for your life, and He wants to bless you abundantly and eternally. Your job, simply put, is to trust Him completely in good times and trying times. And when you're anxious or afraid, pay more attention to God and less attention to your fears. Just do your best, and trust Him to do the rest.

98

UNDERSTANDING MENTAL ILLNESS

UNDERSTANDING THE PROBLEM AND SEEKING TREATMENT

Wisdom shouts in the streets. She cries out in the public square. She calls to the crowds along the main street, to those gathered in front of the city gate: "How long, you simpletons, will you insist on being simpleminded? How long will you mockers relish your mocking? How long will you fools hate knowledge? Come and listen to my counsel. I'll share my heart with you and make you wise."

PROVERBS 1:20–23 NLT

If you've experienced prolonged periods of severe anxiety, debilitating panic, or irrational fear, you may be wondering if you'll ever recover. Perhaps you've tried to solve the problem on your own, without much success. If so, you may have convinced yourself that your condition is permanent. But that sort of negative thinking won't help you find a solution that works for you. So it's now time to replace negativity with a healthy dose of reality. And the truth is simply this: if you understand the problem and seek help, things are going to get better.

Anxiety disorders are so common, and so well understood, that a wide range of treatments are readily available. Until you've tried them all you can't honestly say that your condition is permanent or incurable. But in reality, you won't need to try them all because at least one of those treatments will be right for you.

Thankfully, the strategies for treating anxiety and panic disorders are straightforward. And as it turns out, talk therapy or medication or a combination of the two have proven remarkably effective for most sufferers. So if you're feeling helpless or hopeless, it's time to ask for help. Don't give up, don't be discouraged, and don't suffer alone. Instead, keep working with your healthcare professionals until you find the best treatment for you.

MORE THOUGHTS ABOUT MENTAL ILLNESS

We know that mental illness is not something that happens to other people. It touches us all. Why then is mental illness met with so much misunderstanding and fear?
TIPPER GORE

Mental illness is so prevalent. People don't always have the right terms for it, but most families have had a brush with it.
RON HOWARD

Your illness is not your identity.
Your chemistry is not your character.
RICK WARREN

More from God's Word

A wise man will hear, and will increase learning;
and a man of understanding shall attain unto wise counsels.
PROVERBS 1:5 KJV

Morning by morning he wakens me
and opens my understanding to his will.
The Sovereign LORD has
spoken to me, and I have listened.
ISAIAH 50:4–5 NLT

Wisdom and strength belong to God;
counsel and understanding are His.
JOB 12:13 HCSB

A foolish person enjoys doing wrong, but a person
with understanding enjoys doing what is wise.
PROVERBS 10:23 NCV

Who among you is wise and understanding?
Let him show by his good behavior
his deeds in the gentleness of wisdom.
JAMES 3:13 NASB

A Timely Tip

If you or someone you know seems to be overly anxious, dangerously sad, or extremely panicked, don't wait for things to get better on their own. Get help ASAP.

99

WISDOM

TRUST GOD'S WISDOM

The LORD gives wisdom; from His mouth come knowledge and understanding.
PROVERBS 2:6 HCSB

In today's information-driven world, facts, figures, and opinions are just a click away. But real wisdom doesn't come from a search engine or from talk radio or from the evening news or from a Facebook page. Searching for genuine nuggets of wisdom in the endless stream of modern-day media messages is like panning for gold without a pan— only harder. Why? Because real wisdom doesn't come from the world; it comes from God. And it's up to you to ask Him for it. "Ask, and it will be given to you; seek, and you will find; knock, and it will be opened to you. For everyone who asks receives, and he who seeks finds, and to him who knocks it will be opened" (Matthew 7:7–8 NKJV). Jesus made it clear to His disciples that they should petition God to meet their needs. So should you.

Genuine, heartfelt prayer produces powerful changes in you and in your world. When you lift your heart to God, you open yourself to a never-ending source of divine wisdom and infinite love. Yet too many folks are too timid or too pessimistic to ask God for help. Please don't count yourself among their number.

God will give you wisdom if you have the courage to ask Him (and the determination to keep asking Him). If you call upon Him, He will give you guidance and perspective. If you make God's priorities your priorities, He will lead you along a path of His choosing. If you study God's teachings, you will be reminded that God's reality is the ultimate reality.

As you accumulate wisdom, you may feel the need to share your insights with friends and family members. If so, remember this: your actions must reflect the values that you hold dear. The best way to share your wisdom—perhaps the only way—is not by your words but by your example.

MORE THOUGHTS ABOUT GOD'S WISDOM

Knowledge is horizontal. Wisdom is vertical; it comes down from above.
BILLY GRAHAM

Wisdom is the power to see and the inclination to choose the best and highest goal, together with the surest means of attaining it.
J. I. PACKER

True wisdom is marked by willingness to listen and a sense of knowing when to yield.
ELIZABETH GEORGE

Wisdom is the right use of knowledge. To know is not to be wise. There is no fool so great as the knowing fool. But, to know how to use knowledge is to have wisdom.

C. H. SPURGEON

MORE FROM GOD'S WORD

But the wisdom that is from above is first pure, then peaceable, gentle, willing to yield, full of mercy and good fruits, without partiality and without hypocrisy.

JAMES 3:17 NKJV

But if any of you lacks wisdom, let him ask of God, who gives to all generously and without reproach, and it will be given to him.

JAMES 1:5 NASB

He that walketh with wise men shall be wise: but a companion of fools shall be destroyed.

PROVERBS 13:20 KJV

Get wisdom—how much better it is than gold! And get understanding—it is preferable to silver.

PROVERBS 16:16 HCSB

A TIMELY TIP

Need wisdom? God's got it and He wants you to acquire it. If you want the same thing, then study His Word and associate with godly people.

100

WORRY

TAKE YOUR WORRIES TO GOD, AND LEAVE THEM THERE

Therefore do not worry about tomorrow,
for tomorrow will worry about its own things.
Sufficient for the day is its own trouble.
MATTHEW 6:34 NKJV

Because we are fallible human beings struggling through the inevitable challenges of life here on earth, we worry. Even though we, as Christians, have been promised the gift of eternal life—even though we are blessed by God's love and protection—we find ourselves fretting over the inevitable frustrations of everyday life.

Where is the best place to take your worries? Take them to God. Take your concerns to Him; take your fears to Him; take your doubts to Him; take your weaknesses to Him; take your sorrows to Him . . . and leave them all there. Seek protection from the Creator and build your spiritual house upon the Rock that cannot be moved. Remind yourself that God still sits in His heaven and that you are His beloved child. Then, perhaps, you will worry less and trust Him a more. And that's as it should be because the Lord is trustworthy, and you are protected.

Perhaps you are concerned about your future, your relationships, or your finances. Or perhaps you are simply a "worrier" by nature. If so, choose to make Matthew 6:34 a regular part of your daily Bible reading. This beautiful verse will remind you to live in day-tight compartments and to leave everything else up to God.

MORE THOUGHTS ABOUT WORRY

Worry is the senseless process of cluttering up tomorrow's opportunities with leftover problems from today.
BARBARA JOHNSON

Worry is a cycle of inefficient thoughts whirling around a center of fear.
CORRIE TEN BOOM

Too many people worry, but don't do anything about it.
PEARL BAILEY

Knowing that God is faithful really helps me to not be captivated by worry.
JOSH MCDOWELL

Pray, and let God worry.
MARTIN LUTHER

Do not worry about tomorrow. This is not a suggestion, but a command.
SARAH YOUNG

MORE FROM GOD'S WORD

Cast your burden on the LORD, and He shall sustain you;
He shall never permit the righteous to be moved.
PSALM 55:22 NKJV

Let not your heart be troubled;
you believe in God, believe also in Me.
JOHN 14:1 NKJV

Do not be anxious about anything,
but in every situation, by prayer and petition,
with thanksgiving, present your requests to God.
PHILIPPIANS 4:6 NIV

Peace I leave with you; My peace I give to you;
not as the world gives do I give to you.
Do not let your heart be troubled, nor let it be fearful.
JOHN 14:27 NASB

Trust the LORD your God with all your heart
and lean not on your own understanding; in all your ways
submit to him, and he will make your paths straight.
PROVERBS 3:5–6 NIV

A TIMELY TIP

Divide your areas of concern into two categories: those you can control and those you can't. Focus on the former and refuse to waste time or energy worrying about the latter. You have worries, but God has solutions. Your challenge is to trust Him to solve the problems that are simply too big for you to resolve on your own.

RECOGNIZING COMMON MOOD AND ANXIETY DISORDERS

COMMON ANXIETY AND MOOD DISORDERS

An anxiety disorder is a condition that causes exaggerated emotions to interfere with a person's ability to lead a normal life. All of us feel anxious from time to time, but a person who experiences an anxiety disorder is faced with overwhelming, debilitating feelings of fear, dread, or panic. Obsessive behaviors—characterized by recurrent, unwanted thoughts (obsessions) or undesirable repetitive behaviors (compulsions)—are also considered to be anxiety-related conditions.

A mood disorder is a mental health condition that has an adverse effect on a person's emotional state. The two most common mood disorders are depression and bipolar disorder. Both of these conditions are further divided into subcategories based, in part, on the severity and duration of the person's symptoms.

Mood and anxiety disorders are quite common. The National Institute of Mental Health (NIMH) estimates that almost 10 percent of US adults will experience a mood disorder during a given year and that over 20 percent of adults will experience a mood disorder sometime during their lifetime.

Anxiety disorders are even more common than mood disorders. In fact, the NIMH calls anxiety disorders "the most common mental health concern in the United States." They estimate that currently about 40 million adults (almost 20 percent of the adult population) suffer from some type of anxiety-related condition. Common anxiety disorders include, but are not limited to, generalized anxiety disorder, obsessive-compulsive disorder, panic disorder, post-traumatic stress disorder, and social anxiety disorder.

Both mood and anxiety disorders tend to run in families, which means that they can be inherited from one or both parents. Additionally, environmental factors—such as a traumatic event, a serious illness, or a significant life-changing situation—can be causal factors.

Clearly mood and anxiety disorders pose serious problems for individual sufferers and for the loved ones who care for them. Thankfully, these disorders are, in most cases, readily treatable with therapy or medication—or a combination of the two—combined with self-care.

The following descriptions provide a brief introduction to the above-mentioned disorders. If you need to learn more, detailed information is readily available. And if you suspect that you or someone you care about may be impacted by one of these disorders, or by a mental illness not mentioned here, don't wait to seek treatment. Mental health problems can evolve into serious, debilitating, life-threatening conditions. So it's always better to seek professional guidance sooner rather than later.

THE MOST COMMON ANXIETY DISORDERS

Generalized Anxiety Disorder (GAD): This condition is characterized by chronic anxiety, by exaggerated worry, tension, and apprehension even when there is no discernable cause for those feelings.

GAD, which often begins in the teen years or early adulthood, develops slowly. According to NIMH, symptoms of GAD include the following:

- Being excessively worried about everyday things
- Having trouble controlling worries or feelings of nervousness
- Knowing that one's worries are exaggerated and excessive
- Feeling restless; having trouble relaxing
- Difficulty concentrating
- Being easily startled
- Having trouble falling asleep or staying asleep
- Feeling tired most or all of the time
- Experiencing physical symptoms such as headaches, muscle aches, stomachaches, or unexplained pains
- Difficulty swallowing
- Twitches or tremors
- Being irritable or feeling "on edge"
- Sweating profusely, feeling lightheaded or out of breath

Children and teens with GAD often worry excessively about:
- Performances in school, sports, or other public activities
- Catastrophes such as earthquakes or wars

Adults with GAD are often highly nervous about everyday circumstances, such as:
- Job security or performance
- Health
- Finances
- The health and well-being of their children
- Being late
- Completing household chores and other responsibilities

Post-traumatic Stress Disorder (PTSD): This disorder develops in some people who have either experienced or witnessed a terrifying, life-threatening, or life-altering event. PTSD symptoms may start within one month of the traumatic event, but for many individuals, symptoms may not appear until years later. These symptoms create significant problems in social settings, work-related environments, and relationships. PTSD symptoms are generally grouped into four categories: intrusive memories, avoidance, negative changes in thinking and mood, and changes in physical and emotional reactions.

Obsessive-Compulsive Disorder (OCD): This anxiety disorder is characterized by recurrent, unwanted thoughts (obsessions) and/or repetitive behaviors (compulsions). Repetitive behaviors such as hand washing, counting, checking, or cleaning are often performed with the hope of preventing obsessive thoughts or making those thoughts go away. Performing these rituals, however, provides only temporary relief. Not performing the aforementioned repetitive behaviors causes psychological discomfort and a marked increase in anxiety.

Panic Disorder: This anxiety disorder is characterized by unexpected and repeated episodes of intense fear (panic attacks) accompanied by physical and psychological symptoms that include:
- Sudden and repeated panic attacks that result in overwhelming feelings of anxiety and fear
- The feeling of being out of control
- The fear of death or impending doom during a panic attack
- Physical symptoms during a panic attack, such as a pounding or racing heart, sweating, chills, trembling, breathing problems, weakness or dizziness, tingly or numb hands, chest pain, stomach pain, or nausea
- An intense worry about when the next panic attack will occur
- A fear or avoidance of places where panic attacks have occurred in the past

Social Anxiety Disorder (also known as Social Phobia): This disorder is characterized by excessive self-consciousness and overwhelming anxiety resulting from social or performance situations in which the person is exposed to unfamiliar people or to possible scrutiny by others. A person with social phobia fears that he or she may act in a way—or may display anxiety-related symptoms—that will cause embarrassment or humiliation. In extreme cases, the phobia may be so broad that the sufferer experiences symptoms almost anytime he or she interacts with other people.

THE MOST COMMON MOOD DISORDERS

Major Depression (also known as Major Depressive Disorder or Clinical Depression): Major depression is a common, serious mood disorder. It causes severe symptoms that affect how one feels, thinks, and manages daily activities such as sleeping, eating, or working. To be diagnosed with depression, symptoms must be present for at least two weeks. Symptoms include, but are not limited to:

- Feelings of sadness, hopelessness, or despondency
- Feelings of guilt, worthlessness, or helplessness
- Difficulty sleeping, early-morning awakening, or oversleeping
- Having noticeably less interest in usual pleasurable activities
- Decreased energy level
- Appetite or weight changes
- Feeling that life no longer has meaning
- Irritability
- Moving or talking more slowly
- Feeling restless or having trouble sitting still
- Difficulty concentrating, remembering, or making decisions

- Thoughts of death or suicide, or suicide attempts
- Aches or pains, headaches, cramps, or digestive problems that have no clear physical cause

Bipolar Disorder (also known as Manic-Depressive Disorder): According to NIMH, bipolar disorder is "a brain disorder that causes unusual shifts in mood, energy, activity levels, and the ability to carry out day-to-day tasks." People suffering with this condition experience episodes of depression alternating with periods of mania.

There are four basic types of bipolar disorder, all of which involve demonstrable changes in mood, energy, and activity levels. These moods vacillate between periods of extreme energy and/or irritability (known as manic episodes) followed by periods of extreme sadness, hopelessness, or despair (known as depressive episodes). According to NIMH, people experiencing manic episodes may exhibit some or most of the following symptoms:

MANIC SYMPTOMS IN BIPOLAR DISORDER

- Feeling very "up," "high," or elated
- Feeling extremely energetic
- Increased activity levels
- Feeling jumpy or "wired"
- Trouble falling asleep or staying asleep
- Exhibiting pressured speech patterns, i.e., talking faster than normal
- Feeling agitated, irritable, or "touchy"
- Racing thoughts
- Attempting to do many things at once

According to NIMH, bipolar patients experiencing depressive episodes may exhibit some or most of the following symptoms:

DEPRESSIVE SYMPTOMS IN BIPOLAR DISORDER

- Feeling very sad, down, empty, or hopeless
- Having very little energy
- Exhibiting decreased activity levels
- Trouble sleeping (either too little sleep or too much)
- Feeling unable to enjoy anything
- Feeling worried and empty
- Trouble concentrating
- Forgetfulness
- Eating too much or too little
- Feeling tired or "slowed down"
- Thinking about death or suicide

OTHER COMMON MOOD DISORDERS

Persistent Depressive Disorder (also known as Dysthymia): This is a chronic, low-grade mood disorder in which symptoms of depression or irritability last for at least two years. A person diagnosed with persistent depressive disorder may experience episodes of major depression along with periods of less severe symptoms. But for a diagnosis of persistent depressive disorder, the depressive symptoms—both major symptoms and less severe ones—must last, in total, for at least two years.

Postpartum Depression: Many women feel mildly depressed or anxious after the birth of a child. These symptoms, if they occur at all, typically clear within two weeks after delivery. Postpartum depression is a much more serious condition. Women with postpartum depression experience full-blown major depression after delivery. Feelings of extreme sadness, anxiety, and exhaustion are common, thus making it difficult for mothers to care for themselves and their babies.

Seasonal Affective Disorder (SAD): This is a form of depression that occurs during certain seasons of the year. Typically SAD begins in the late autumn or early winter and lasts until spring or summer. Less commonly, SAD episodes may begin during the late spring or summer. Symptoms of winter seasonal affective disorder often resemble those of major depression.

A FINAL NOTE

For previous generations, mental illness was often spoken about in whispers. For many sufferers and their families, emotional disorders were a source of embarrassment or shame. Thankfully, this is no longer the case. Today, mental health is a top-of-mind priority for medical professionals who are keenly aware that most mental disorders have both medical as well as psychological origins. As such, most emotional disorders are now eminently treatable. Thanks to advances in medical science, healing is available through counseling, through medication, or through a combination of the two.

If you suspect that you—or someone you care about—may be experiencing a mood disorder, an anxiety disorder, or any other psychiatric condition, don't hesitate to seek professional help. To fully experience God's abundance, you need to be spiritually and emotionally healthy. If mental health professionals can help you achieve the emotional stability you need to experience God's abundance here on earth, you should consider your treatment to be part of God's plan for your life.